T0354728

WHAT IS HOLINESS?

BEING ONE WITH GOD AND GOD'S PEOPLE

THOMAS VAN DYKE

ARCHWAY
PUBLISHING

Archway Publishing books may be ordered through booksellers or by contacting:

Archway Publishing
1663 Liberty Drive
Bloomington, IN 47403
www.archwaypublishing.com
844-669-3957

Scripture quotations marked KJV are from the Holy Bible, King James Version (Authorized Version). First published in 1611. Quoted from the KJV Classic Reference Bible, Copyright © 1983 by The Zondervan Corporation.

ISBN: 978-1-6657-5839-0 (sc)
ISBN: 978-1-6657-5840-6 (e)

Library of Congress Control Number: 2024906191

Print information available on the last page.

Archway Publishing rev. date: 03/25/2024

CONTENTS

IN MEMORY

I want to dedicate this book to the memory of Ed and Sue Osenga, who showed me the reality of holiness in their marriage and their love for God. Ed and Sue died during the writing of this book after 70 years of marriage, but they left an indelible imprint on my life concerning the power of holiness.

ACKNOWLEDGMENTS

I want to express my deep gratitude to my son, Dr Michael Van Dyke Ph.D., for doing the editing of this book. It is not only his editing expertise but his broad knowledge of cultural, philosophical, and theological information that helped shape the content and character of this book. I would also like to express my thanks to my grandson, Caleb Van Dyke, who designed the cover to express my concept of holiness.

INTRODUCTION

The concept of holiness is one of the significant topics and one of the most critical ideas in the Bible. Yet, I have concluded that it is one of the most misunderstood concepts of the Bible. The Bible states that holiness is an attribute of God and must be an attribute of humans– "be ye holy as I am holy." The Bible tells us that because He is holy, we should fear Him on the one hand and worship Him on the other. If I open my iPad and ask Siri to give me a definition of "holiness," I get "the state of being holy," or "a title given to the Pope, Orthodox patriarchs, and the Dalai Lama, or used in addressing them." Another I get is "a mid-19th century movement among Methodists in the US, emphasizing the Wesleyan doctrine of the sanctification of believers." If I ask Siri for a definition of "holy," I get "dedicated to God or a religious purpose, sacred, a person devoted to the service of God," or "morally and spiritually excellent." As I have searched Christian literature, I have found at least six different explanations of holiness. I am sure there are more. The Bible declares that, without holiness, we will not see God. That should immediately elevate it to the top of our "must-have" list. But what is it? The Bible says that it is beautiful, scary, a mystery, a characteristic of God, and a needed aspect of humans, but it does not explain its essence—or does it?

Paul attempts to show the essence of holiness in Ephesians by likening the relationship of Christ and the church to a marriage between husband and wife. If we view the first marriage- that of Adam and Eve- as the perfect marriage since there was no sin, we can also say that that marriage was holy. But, again, what does that mean? The writer of Genesis explains it this way:

"And Adam said, this *is* now bone of my bones and flesh of my flesh: she shall be called woman because she was taken out of man. Therefore shall a man leave his father and his mother, and shall cleave unto his wife: and they shall be one flesh. And they were both naked, the man and his wife, and were not ashamed." (Gen 2:23-25)

That holy marriage exemplified (1) a pure, perfect, and complete identification with each other, working as *one flesh* or body, and (2) a transparent and *naked* relationship in which there were no secrets. It is these two characteristics that, I believe, define holiness, whether it is with God or with another person, as in the case of marriage.

Another word often used with holiness is "sanctify," meaning to set apart or declare holy. One can use it both to set oneself apart in holiness to another person or to draw another person into a holy relationship with you. e.g., "And for their sakes, I sanctify myself, that they also might be sanctified through the truth. (Joh 17:19)

After the fall or separation, that sense of holiness in the garden disappeared. Eve, who was "bone of my bone, and flesh of my flesh," to Adam became "that woman," and God, who was someone to walk and talk with, became someone to be feared and from whom to hide. Immediately, God had to set in motion a plan to restore that state of holiness between Himself and humanity if human beings were to survive. (Gen 3:15) His plan is the "Gospel," or the atoning work of Christ. It is good news because it is the only way to reestablish that holy relationship between humans and God. Without it, there is no hope of people genuinely getting along or seeing God (Heb 12:14). Paul states in Ephesians that holiness is a great mystery in marriage and the Church (Eph 5:31,32).

When I began writing this book, there was a married couple in my community for whom I have the highest respect and admiration. Unfortunately, they have both passed away since. Ed was ninety-one years old then, and Sue was eighty-eight, and they had been married for seventy years. I sensed something foreign to many households when

I walked into their home. It was a sense of love, respect, commitment, oneness, and pure enjoyment of each other. They could not stop talking about each other and seemed to light up when they were in each other's presence. In public, they would hold hands and beam when they looked at each other as if they were still twenty-one and eighteen-year-old newlyweds. Young people seeing them were warmed – if not embarrassed – by their fearless show of affection for each other. Seventy years before, Ed and Sue sanctified themselves in marriage to each other for better or worse, for richer or for poorer, in sickness and health, till parted by death. They never reneged on that commitment. That unwavering commitment changed their lives in a way they never envisioned. They became kinder, more accommodating, forgiving, accepting, loving, willing to endure difficult times, more inclined to be transparent with each other, and more willing to share all their possessions. Ed and Sue displayed my concept of holiness in their marriage, so I am dedicating this book to them.

Holiness is a complete, pure, and undying commitment of oneness and unity to each other and God. It is that lasting commitment to holiness that, by its very nature, can produce righteousness in humanity on all levels. Ed and Sue were not perfectly sinless when they spoke their vows to each other and were not perfectly innocent after seventy years of marriage. However, they would both tell you that they were not the same people who stood at the altar seventy years before because of their commitment to holiness in their marriage. Paul echoes that same idea in Philippians, chapter three, where he says he is on a journey toward God's high calling but isn't there yet. God has never asked for our righteousness but our holiness – "You are my people, and I am your God." In that atmosphere of holiness, He is free to conform us to His righteousness.

In this book, I intend first to explore the mystery of holiness. I will give you a broad outline of holiness in the first chapter and go into more detail in the following chapters. I will also explore the relationship between holiness and righteousness.

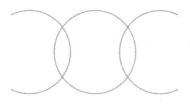

THE NATURE OF HOLINESS

"And thou shalt love the Lord thy God with all thy heart, and with all thy soul, and with all thy mind, and with all thy strength: this *is* the first commandment. And the second *is* like, *namely* this, Thou shalt love thy neighbor as thyself. There is none other commandment greater than these." (Mar 12:30,31)

The Bible teaches that we have two critical relationships in life: a "vertical" one with God and a "horizontal" one with other people. Both are equally important in the eyes of God.

"If a man say, I love God, and hateth his brother, he is a liar: for he that loveth not his brother whom he hath seen, how can he love God whom he hath not seen?" (1Jn 4:20)

John says in the above verses that both relationships must be loving relationships in which the participants are not just *aware* of each other but have each other's best interests at heart. They are relationships in which participants are committed to uniting and working for a common good. I believe that these relationships are what God is talking about when He says, "Be holy, for I am holy." This concept will be the theme I will explore in this book.

In its strictest (vertical) sense, holiness means being set apart for perfect and complete unity with God. Jesus demonstrated this lifestyle as He walked this earth as a man. John quotes Jesus as saying, "I and *my* Father are one" (John 10:30) and "...I do nothing of myself; but as my Father hath taught me, I speak these things." (Joh 8:28) In holiness, we submit ourselves to God's will, saying, "Father...not my will, but thine, be done" (Luk 22:42). We must build our lives on this rock-solid foundation of holiness with God if we want to weather the storms of life and not be destroyed by them (Matt 7:24,25).

On the horizontal level, Christ instructs us to love others as ourselves and do unto them as you would have them do unto you. We must treat others with the same respect and compassion we have for ourselves. Indeed, this is the first step in establishing a holy relationship. However, I believe there is a second step that is as critical as the first. That is the step of *commitment*. The prophet Amos asks, "How can two walk together unless they agree" (to walk together)? (Amos 3:3; emphasis mine) The most well-known example of a holy relationship on earth is the bond two enter through marriage. They commit to each other "for better, or for worse, in sickness and in health, for richer or poorer, till death do us part." Each has a role to perform in that union, which complements the other and enables the marriage union to function despite future difficulties. Paul uses the analogy of marriage in the fifth chapter of Ephesus to help clarify the holy relationship between Christ and the church. I will discuss these in more detail in later chapters.

But to take things a step further, it would seem God has designed all living organisms to exhibit perfect harmony between parts and the whole. We see it in human and animal life, where all the body's functions, mediated by the brain, are perfectly coordinated. We also see it in plant life, as roots, stalks, branches, and leaves all work together for the plant's growth and propagation. Finally, we can consider the interrelationships between plants and animals, where plants provide oxygen for animal life, and animals provide carbon dioxide for plants. These relationships – between parts and wholes and between wholes- illuminate God's holiness and its implications for human personal and spiritual connections.

In the thirteenth chapter of Corinthians, Paul states that we must maintain three qualities in our relationships with others. I have already mentioned love. The other two are faith and hope. These three spiritual qualities, together, make up the foundation of holiness, just as gravel, cement, and water are the ingredients of a concrete foundation. These qualities are not qualities that we bring to holiness but are attributes of God that we *share* with God as we participate in His divine nature (II Pet 1:4). It is the faith of God, the hope of God, and the charity, or the sacrificial love, of God that gives holiness its great sense of purity and beauty. Only as these qualities of God permeate and flow through us do we experience what it means to be a sanctified and holy child of God.

As we look at the quality of faith, I would like to note that the KJV uses the phrase "faith *of* Jesus," whereas other translations use the phrase "faith *in* Jesus" (Gal 2:16). Both phrases can be technically correct translations; however, I think it is essential to realize that our faith is in Christ and *originates* with Jesus. The writer of Hebrews states:

> "Looking unto Jesus the <u>author and finisher</u> of *our* faith; who for the joy that was set before him endured the cross, despising the shame, and is set down at the right hand of the throne of God." (Heb 12:2 emphasis mine)

The faith of Jesus, authored and completed in us, gives us the capacity to have faith *in* Jesus. Because our faith originates in Christ, faith qualifies as a foundational component of holiness. Paul states that "the just shall live by faith" (Rom 1:17, Gal 3:11, Heb 10:38). To have a holy relationship with God or another person, you must have faith in the truth and viability of what they have said or promised, to the point that you will act on it. It isn't reasonable to think you can have a holy relationship with someone you can't trust. But learning to trust may take time.

When I married my wife 57 years ago, I didn't realize I had entered that marriage carrying deep betrayal and rejection wounds. As a result, even after we were married, I lived a very independent and self-sufficient life, burying myself in work. I committed my life to three different professions at one time— school principal, pastor, and photo lab technician.

To put it mildly, my family suffered. My wife eventually reached a point where she cried out to God, telling him that because He put us together, she would not divorce me, but that she did feel like dying. It became a turning point in our marriage when she finally dared to tell me about her conversation with God and how miserable she felt. I finally realized the pain she was going through because of her devotion to me. Her honesty opened my eyes to the fact that she was a woman I could fully trust. She would never leave me or forsake me. That experience was one of the great healing experiences of my life, and as a result, the foundation of holiness began to grow in our marriage. The same thing is valid on a spiritual level; we will not walk in holiness with God unless we wake up to the fact that God is entirely trustworthy.

As faith describes our daily walk, hope describes the goal of our spiritual journey. The writer of Hebrews states that "faith is the substance of things hoped for" (Heb 11:1). Put another way, our acts of faith are steps taken on a road that we expect will lead us to the desired goal. In the next chapter, Hebrews 12:2, the writer states that God, the Father, showed His Son a road that would end in the joy of being seated at the Father's right hand. As Jesus viewed this goal– the joy set before Him – He submitted to his Father and went to the cross in faith. It was that step of faith that demonstrated the holiness of their relationship. However, without focusing on the hope or expectation God has given us, we might find it impossible to ever walk with God in holiness because hope gives us the patience to persevere. Paul says in Romans that the "God of hope" will always give us an expectation of joy and peace as we walk in holiness with Him.

> "Now the God of hope fill you with all joy and peace
> in believing, that ye may abound in hope, through the
> power of the Holy Ghost." (Rom 15:13)

The last and most crucial ingredient of holiness is love. The first two ingredients describe how we receive grace from God and others as we walk in holiness with them. Charity has more to do with *giving ourselves to* God and others. Holiness is a two-way street. We receive by faith, but we give to others by love. Faith cannot work by itself, and true charity cannot. Paul states that if we have the faith to move mountains but have not love, we are nothing (I Cor 13:2). He also says that we can believe we are acting in love when, in reality, we are not (vs. 3). True "agape" love, or charity, is not just an act of generosity; it is a giving of ourselves as a sacrifice *to* God *for* others. (Eph 5:2) Only when an act of charity flows out of one's total submission to God through faith can it be considered a holy act of true charity. I intend to enlarge upon this point later.

Love is also expressed in a strong desire to help others succeed. In Psalm 37:4, the psalmist says, "Delight thyself also in the Lord: and he shall give thee the desires of thine heart." We find genuine delight in a relationship, not only when we are getting our needs and desires fulfilled but also when we are meeting the needs and fulfilling the desires of others. God truly wants to provide us with the desires of our hearts, but as I have said, holiness is a two-way street. True holiness grows in our relationship with God when we delight in giving God what *He* desires and having Him fulfill our desires.

The last thing I would like to explain about holiness is that it has two phases. The first phase is the initial *commitment* to walking in holiness with God. It is much like a wedding. At a wedding, two people promise to forsake all others and give themselves only to each other as long as they live. It is a commitment to marital holiness and is a time of hope and excitement. In the spiritual realm, the "wedding," or in the Jewish sense, the betrothal, is when we accept Christ's invitation (the gospel) to walk with Him in holiness.

Our motivation for accepting Christ's invitation should be that we have an opportunity to be wedded to the creator of the universe. We can walk and talk with Him in much the same way Adam did before the separation. He invites us to a life of hope and fulfillment that we may have only dreamed about. Sadly, today's evangelistic message has often become a message of fear and threats of hell rather than an invitation to peace and joy, which only holiness can produce. Evangelists urge us to participate in "shotgun weddings" rather than something entered into through love. When people accept Christ as their "personal savior," I hope they will not consider that commitment merely a "get out of hell free" card but rather as accepting God's invitation to walk with Him in personal holiness.

The second phase is the actual walking out of holiness. Paul describes this in Gal 5:25, where he states that if we live in the spirit, we should walk in the spirit. We soon realize that marriage is not just a matter of living happily ever after. It requires that a couple walk together in the reality of holiness daily. When both husband and wife commit to holiness, an atmosphere of compassion and forgiveness arises in which couples are free to face their flaws and hurts. Holiness in a relationship provides a safe atmosphere for a couple to expose and deal with any weaknesses that could destroy them and their marriage. If couples suppress their faults instead of dealing with them honestly and openly, they will not find healing in their relationship. Also, they will never experience the pure joy that holiness can bring their marriage.

In John's first letter to the churches, he describes our holiness with God as a time of sweet fellowship in which we can acknowledge our faults, be forgiven, and be cleansed from the guilt damaging our lives.

> "This then is the message which we have heard of him, and declare unto you, that God is light, and in him is no darkness at all. If we say that we have fellowship with him, and walk in darkness, we lie, and do not the truth: but if we walk in the light, as he is in the light, we have fellowship one with another, and the blood of Jesus Christ his Son cleanseth us from all sin. If we say that we have no sin, we deceive ourselves, and the truth is not in us. If we confess our sins, he is faithful and just to forgive us *our* sins and to cleanse us from all unrighteousness."
>
> (1Jn 1:5-9)

Forgiveness and cleansing of sin are two of the most significant benefits of holiness for the believer. Having dealt with sin through walking in holiness, one dares to approach God's throne of grace and share His power in our daily lives. Holiness with God must be the top priority in our lives because, without it, we will never experience the joy, peace, and freedom from sin that God has promised us through His grace.

"but as he who called you is holy, you also be holy in all your conduct,"

(1Pe 1:15 ERV)

"Follow peace with all *men,* and holiness, without which no man shall see the Lord:"

(Heb 12:14)

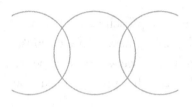

CHAPTER 2

THE HISTORY OF HOLINESS

Holiness starts with God. God is naturally "holy" (Rev 4:8; I Pet 1:16) and righteous. These two qualities of God are closely related but not the same. Holiness describes God's perfect union with Himself within the Trinity and also the harmonious relationship He desires to have with His creation. Righteousness, on a human level, describes a just and equitable behavior that promotes and maintains a sense of community or oneness among people. On a spiritual level, righteousness is a behavior that aligns with God's rightness. Separated from God, we cannot adequately perform either standard of righteousness. Only through holiness with God (God in me and I in God) will God achieve both standards of righteousness in and through us.

The Bible introduces the idea of holiness in the first chapter of Genesis, where we read that God said, " Let **us** make man in **our** image, after **our** likeness" (Gen 1:26, emphasis mine). We also see phrases such as "God said" (Gen 1: 3,5,9,11,14,24,26), "the Spirit of God moved" (Gen 1:2), and "all things were created by (Christ)" (Col 1:16 emphasis mine). These phrases point to the creation as a joint activity of all three members of the Trinity operating in perfect unity and harmony. In other words, creation was an act that reflected the holiness of God: Father, Spirit, and Son.

Next, we read about a garden. The Bible says that after God created

Adam out of the dust of the earth, he breathed life into him and placed him in the Garden of Eden to tend it (Gen 2:15).

The creation of the first man required a two-step process. First, God created a physical body from the dust of the earth. This part of the creation would indicate that God wanted this man to be a physical being that could interact with the material world. Then, He breathed His life or spirit into Adam so that God's created man, as a spirit, could interact with Him. So, in essence, Adam was a spirit man living in a physical body and, as such, could now walk in unity or holiness with God as he functioned in this world.

Then God created Eve to be Adam's helper, not out of the dust of the earth, but out of Adam. Therefore, just as God could see Adam as part of Himself, Adam could look at Eve as part of himself– bone of his bones and flesh of his flesh (Gen 2:23). Paul would later echo that concept when he said that a man who loves his wife loves himself (Eph 5:28). Though the scripture doesn't specify, I believe Eve not only received a physical body through Adam but also received the spirit or life of God that was in him. This action does not suggest a hierarchy of the sexes; instead, I believe it implies equality of males and females. They are the same stuff. Also, just as God saw Adam as part of Himself, Adam now saw Eve as part of Himself. So God placed the man and woman together in the garden to "dress it and to keep it." At this point, we could ask a legitimate question. How did Adam and Eve know how to care for the garden? Did God create that knowledge in them when He formed them? The story doesn't say. However, Adam and Eve were "one" with each other and God; fortunately, God knew everything about gardens. This arrangement typifies holiness in that all three acted as one, not unlike the Holy Trinity. But unfortunately, things didn't stay this way.

So, what happened to destroy that perfect holiness in the garden? Was it not that Satan duped the garden couple into thinking that knowing right from wrong (having a moral conscience) was a more attractive and satisfying way to manage the garden than through a holy relationship with God?

"And when the woman saw that the tree (of knowledge
of good and evil) *was good for food* and that it *was pleasant to the eyes*, and a tree to be desired *to make one wise*,
she took of the fruit thereof and did eat, and gave also
unto her husband with her, and he did eat." (Gen 3:6,
emphasis mine).

In other words, she saw a moral conscience as helping her satisfy her
physical needs (tasted good), appealing to her aesthetic desires (looked
good), and empowering her intellectual prowess (would make her wise).
You may say, "What's wrong with that? Those qualities are outstanding
and attractive." The issue is not whether those qualities are attractive or
unattractive but whether they take the place of God in our lives. Note
what the Apostle John says concerning these three qualities.

"Love not the world, neither the things *that are* in the
world. If any man love the world, the love of the Father
is not in him. "For all that *is* in the world, the lust of the
flesh (tastes good), and the lust of the eyes (looks good),
and the pride of life (wisdom—I can do it.), is not of the
Father, but is of the world." (I Jn 2:15,16 emphasis mine)

In addition to the danger of supplanting God, another subtle threat
is inherent within a moral conscience. Eve did not realize that when a
person violates their moral conscience, the conscience becomes a virtual
tyrant. It fills us with guilt and shame, the two most dangerous conscience levels of the human mind. They will cause us to hide our faults
rather than deal with them (Jn 3:19,20), destroy our faith in God (I Tim
1:19), and eventually destroy us. God warned Adam that if they ate of
the tree, they would surely die (Gen 2:17). It was not that God would
kill them, but that the guilt would. Today, it is accepted in the mental
health field that guilt and shame are the empowering forces behind most,
if not all, sicknesses and early death. Unfortunately, most people today
still believe that managing their lives with a moral conscience is more attractive than holiness, even though God says it will kill them. Many still

shrink from the idea that waiting on God to direct their lives through holiness is a superior concept to any other means they can conceive. As a result of Satan's delusion, humanity has suffered.

Adam and Eve ceased to function based on their oneness with God. Because of that, they no longer felt safe walking and talking with Him; instead, they hid from him because of their guilt and the resulting fear of Him. Hiding from God, in turn, separated them from the wisdom of God and power. They would be inept at managing the garden without that wisdom and power. Therefore, God had to remove them from it. Labor, which once took only a word to accomplish, now would require much sweat. Remember how, when Christ walked this earth, he could speak to the wind, the waves, trees, dead bodies, and mountains, and they would all obey. It was not because he was God but because, as a man, he walked in perfect holiness with his Father.

At this point, I realize you may have questions such as: Are you implying that we could do the same things as Christ if we walked in holiness, or would we cease physical labor? So first, let me say that Christ also did physical work, but He was not limited to physical labor. He also did supernatural work (the Father's work). So, for example, in healing the lame man at the pool, He declared:

> "Verily, verily, I say unto you, The Son can do nothing of himself, but what he seeth the Father do: for what things soever He doeth, these also doeth the Son likewise. (Joh 5:19)

As with Christ, we must do physical labor, but we are not limited to physical abilities. I stated earlier that we are spirit beings living in a physical body. Therefore, we can and must do physical work. However, being spiritual beings, we can also do spiritual work. Consider the following scriptures.

> "Verily, verily, I say unto you, He that believeth on me, the works that I do shall he do also; and greater *works*

than these shall he do; because I go unto my Father."
(Joh 14:12)

"Then he called his twelve disciples together and gave
them power and authority over all devils, and to cure
diseases." (Luk 9:1)

"Now there are diversities of gifts, but the same Spirit.
And there are differences of administrations, but the
same Lord. And there are diversities of operations, but it
is the same God which worketh all in all. But the manifestation of the Spirit is given to every man to profit
withal. For to one is given by the Spirit the word of
wisdom; to another the word of knowledge by the same
Spirit; To another faith by the same Spirit; to another
the gifts of healing by the same Spirit; To another the
working of miracles; to another prophecy; to another
discerning of spirits; to another *divers* kinds of tongues;
to another the interpretation of tongues: But all these
worketh that one and the selfsame Spirit, dividing to
every man severally as he will." (I Cor 12:4-11)

Today, these supernatural works can and should function in the
Church as the body of Christ on this earth. But sadly, some in the
Christian Church teach that we no longer need to utilize miracles since
we have the completed Bible. The above scripture, however, does not
support that belief. However, it says that the Spirit does not give these
gifts for us to administer at our discretion. It is not that every person can
do every spiritual work in their "own" power but that the Holy Spirit
disperses these spiritual abilities throughout the Church as He sees fit. It
is the Holy Spirit that does the miracle. We are only the vehicle through
which He works. I will explain that principle in detail in the next chapter, "The Parable of the Hose." The Church can only use these gifts as
we walk holily with God.

Walking in holiness was, and still is, God's plan for managing the earth. In the eighth chapter of Romans, we find a very enlightening passage of scripture that presents the perspective of creation on this issue. Paul writes,

> "For I reckon that the sufferings of this present time *are* not worthy *to be compared* with the glory which shall be revealed in us. For the earnest expectation of the creature waiteth for the manifestation of the sons of God. For the creature was made subject to vanity, not willingly, but by reason of him who hath subjected *the same* in hope. Because the creature itself also shall be delivered from the bondage of corruption into the glorious liberty of the children of God. For we know that the whole creation groaneth and travaileth in pain together until now." (Rom 8;18-22)

In this passage of scripture, Paul alludes to the fact that people suffer under the burden of physically managing the earth and that the planet is also suffering from this inferior management. It is groaning and travailing in pain until humans get it together, walk in perfect holiness with God, and are again suited to manage the earth properly through the spoken word. We may not see this reality in our lifetime; however, I don't believe we should sit on our hands hoping for a better world after the rapture when we are "fully" redeemed. Instead, we should have the attitude which Paul had when he stated:

> "Not as though I had already attained, either were already perfect: but I follow after, if that I may apprehend that for which also I am apprehended of Christ Jesus. Brethren, I count not myself to have apprehended: but *this* one thing *I do,* forgetting those things which are behind, and reaching forth unto those things which are before, I press toward the mark for the prize of the high calling of God in Christ Jesus. Let us, therefore, as many as be perfect, be thus minded: and if in anything

ye be otherwise minded, God shall reveal even this unto you." (Php3:12-15)

We know that the Holy Spirit performed many miracles through Paul; however, Paul still saw himself as needing to grow toward perfection. Progress in holiness is something we can and should be striving for daily. As in marriage, we must constantly commit ourselves to "walking out" and "apprehending" the reality of our wedding pledge. Paul says:

"Having, therefore, these promises, dearly beloved, let us cleanse ourselves from all filthiness of the flesh and spirit, *perfecting* holiness in the fear of God." (2 Cor 7:1, emphasis mine)

When this happens, the Bible states that:

"The wolf also shall dwell with the lamb, and the leopard shall lie down with the kid; and the calf and the young lion and the fatling together, and a little child shall lead them. And the cow and the bear shall feed; their young ones shall lie down together: and the lion shall eat straw like the ox. And the sucking child shall play on the hole of the asp, and the weaned child shall put his hand on the cockatrice' den. _They shall not hurt_ _nor destroy in all my holy mountain_: for the earth shall be full of the knowledge of the LORD, as the waters cover the sea."

(Isa 11:6-9 emphasis mine)

Since the human race's fall, or more accurately, since its separation from God, people have tried to create relationships that could replace holiness. Somewhere deep within the human psyche, we still carry the notion implanted in us by our Creator that we can do more through unified cooperation than separately. Slogans such as "united we stand," "one for all and all for one," and "the whole is greater than the sum of

the parts" reflect this innate idea. However, without God, these relationships are based on fear – not on a spiritual foundation of faith, hope, and
charity needed in holiness.

Until now, I have not talked much about relationships based on
fear. For example, when Adam and Eve ate the fruit in the garden, the
immediate result was a fear of God. Also, when Cain killed Abel, He
was immediately overcome with the fear that other people would kill
him. Fear, in one form or another, is the most dominating force in the
world. Terrorists use it; advertisers use it; parents use it; politicians use
it; religion uses it; in short, everybody uses it to control and dominate
others. David R. Hawkins, a noted psychiatrist of the 20th century, states,

> "In the energy field of fear, there is the appearance of a
> suppressed energy that has been held throughout life as
> fearfulness. There is a preoccupation with anxiety and
> constant worry about the future. The world looks like a
> frightening place, and a person at that level experiences
> everything in the form of fright.[1]

He also says, "The person who lives in fear projects a punitive, fright-
ening, terrifying image of God."[2]

Without a relationship of holiness with God, the blood covenant
became the most prominent attempt to cope with this fear in almost
all early cultures. In this arrangement, two clans would realize that to
survive, they had to obtain something from the other that they could
not provide, such as defense or food. Therefore, their leaders would enter into a covenant based on two actions. First, each was allowed to ask
the other for something they desired, such as a knife, a spear, a cow, or
even a family member, and this symbolized their willingness to share
something of great value with their covenant partner. Secondly, each
man would cut themselves—usually on the palm of their hand—and clasp
their hands, allowing their blood (symbolizing their lives) to mingle, or

---

[1] Hawkins, David R.. Healing and Recovery (p. 70). Hay House. Kindle Edition.
[2] Hawkins, David R.. Healing and Recovery (p. 31). Hay House. Kindle Edition

would allow their blood to drip into a challis of wine, out of which they would both drink. In each case, they announced they were now one, and each had a legal responsibility to the other. If either person violated the covenant, they would have to die at the hands of someone in their clan. This blood covenant ritual was the primary tool for these cultures to survive and thrive.

According to the Genesis account, God used Abraham's knowledge of the blood covenant as an opportunity to connect with Abraham and eventually with all humanity. First, there was the shedding of blood in chapter fifteen, and then God told Abraham in chapter twenty-two to offer his son Isaac to him as a sacrifice. According to the blood covenant tradition, which Abraham understood, that was legitimate. However, the Bible also says it was to test Abraham. Abraham's willingness to relinquish his son to God–though God provided a substitute ram– would then obligate God to offer him something of equal value–His son– according to the blood covenant. Abraham's action, I believe, opened the door for the "New Covenant" with Abraham's descendants and, eventually, the New Testament Church to return to a holy covenant relationship with God. Christ directed his disciples and the Church to celebrate this covenant until He returned. We call this celebration "Holy Communion." It is a celebration of our return to God in holiness.

As civilization progressed, the use of blood covenants, for the most part, disappeared and was replaced by contracts and treaties. However, none of these brought consequences for breaching them as severely as the blood covenant. Today, very few people are willing to submit themselves to agreements that would force them to live in radical unity and accountability to one another. Instead, most people today prefer to fight for survival rather than unite for survival. Because of this, holiness has become somewhat of an archaic relic in the world and a mysterious quality ascribed to God and various religious activities. Therefore, I think it is necessary to explore the meaning of holiness and how it can work in modern society.

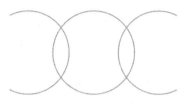

CHAPTER 3

THE PARABLE OF THE HOSE

Several years ago, I was asked to preach the evening services when I was serving as an assistant pastor in a local church. That Sunday afternoon, I struggled to develop a subject for my sermon. I had worked all that week, and I was now desperate for a topic at the eleventh hour. As I prayed desperately for a message, I remembered a saying I learned from one of my mentors. It went like this: "God will always meet your needs; however, sometimes He seems to enjoy "photo finishes." As the finish line came within view (about an hour away), I realized that I was never going to come up with a suitable sermon on my own, and in desperation, I exclaimed, "Lord, I can't do it. If you want me to preach tonight, please give me a topic." Looking back, I now believe that God was waiting for me to reach that point because, almost instantly, the image of a garden hose came into my mind. A garden hose? Really? God also seems to have a great sense of humor.

Nevertheless, I quickly went to my backyard, disconnected the garden hose from the faucet, drained the water, rolled it up, and put it in my car's trunk. When I got to the church, I garnered a few looks as I took the hose from the trunk, dragged it into the church, and laid it on the platform. At least I had their attention—but what now?

In this process, God also placed two scripture verses on my mind. The first was Gal 5:6 ("For in Jesus Christ neither circumcision availeth anything, nor uncircumcision; but faith which worketh by love"), and the second was 2Co 4:7 ("But we have this treasure in earthen vessels, that the excellency of the power may be of God, and not of us"). Armed with only these two verses and a garden hose, I began talking - and a beautiful thing happened. Words began to flow out of my mouth, expressing thoughts I had not thought about or consciously outlined beforehand. I knew the source of this sermon was not me. It came from someone other than me, and I knew it had to be God. I was just being carried along on a wave, like a surfer enjoying the ride's exhilaration. The swell was providing the energy, not me. I wasn't just preaching the message; I was experiencing it. Later, after I shared this message with a missionary group at the church I now attend, a lady came up to me and exclaimed, "I will never look at a hose the same way again."

In the following comparisons, imagine a self-conscious garden hose knowledgeable about certain life principles that so many men and women of God fail to grasp. First, the hose might know it has no purpose or value except what a person assigns it. The hose does not plan and initiate its action apart from a person. If it did, the hose could say such things as "I'm the best hose on the block," "Today I'm going to do this or that," or "I've had some magnificent achievements in my lifetime." No, the only value a hose has is that assigned to it by its owner. It does not function at *its* discretion but rather at the discretion *of* a human being. If it had a mind, it would admit it is nothing without a human being. It has no meaning.

We humans, who do have a sense of "self" and can function at our discretion, *do* tend to think, "I'm the smartest person on the block." or "I'm going to do this or that tomorrow." (see Jas 4:13), or "I have done some great things." Because we perceive our behavior to be ours, we think we have the right and are qualified to plan, carry out, and evaluate our achievements independent of God. We also tend to derive our value from our accomplishments in the world rather than from God. This type of thinking is the complete antithesis of holiness. Holiness asserts that being set apart *for* God, we must carry out all our activities in perfect unity and oneness with God. Paul states it this way: "For of him, and through him, and to him, *are* all things: to whom *be* glory forever.

Amen" (Rom 11:36). I spoke of this perfect unity with God in Chapter 1 when I stated that only when an action flows out of one's total submission to God through holiness can it be considered a holy act and true charity.

As we look at characters in the Bible, God often maneuvered them into a place where they could no longer act independently of Him. They had to work in holiness with God. Consider Abraham. God extracted him from his position of great commercial expertise and prominence in Ur and Haran to a land where he knew little or nothing of how to succeed. Then He let him and his wife age well beyond child-bearing age before telling them they would have a child. Next, we find Joseph in a well and then in jail before God lifted Him to the Egyptian empire's second-highest position. Then we see Moses as the adopted heir of Egyptian royalty, being exiled to the backside of the desert as a common sheepherder before God used him to be his voice to free His people from the grip of slavery. Next, Jonah had to be swallowed by a fish before God could use him as His voice to Nineveh. Next, God had to humble Peter before He could use him as the voice of Pentecost. Finally, we see Saul the Pharisee, who thought he could single-handedly destroy the early Christian church through intimidation and persecution. When God intervened in his life, he exclaimed, "For if a man thinks himself to be something, when he is nothing, he deceives himself" (Gal 6:3). To remind him of that fact, God renamed him Paul, meaning "child" or "little one."

The hose next knows a corollary to the first: it knows that it cannot produce the water that flows through it by itself. The hose is not a water producer but only a water transporter. Water in the Bible often refers to the spiritual life of God (Zoe) provided by the presence of the Holy Spirit in us. Like the hose, we are not the source of our spiritual life, only its container or vessel. Paul says, "... we have this treasure in earthen vessels, that the excellency of the power may be of God, and not of us" (2Co 4:7). John quotes Christ as saying, "The Spirit is the one who gives (Zoe, or spiritual) life, human strength can do nothing" (Jn 6:63 CEV emphasis mine).

In the 15th chapter of John's gospel, John recounts how Jesus taught this principle to His disciples. He took them out to a vineyard to study grapevines. In this story, Jesus likened Himself to the vine of the grape plant and his disciples to the branches. There is only one vine but many branches. Each branch is embedded in the vine, enabling the sap to pass easily from the vine to the branch. The branch cannot produce sap independently but must depend on the vine and root system to provide the sap that flows through it. Once it is in the branch, the sap gives life to the branch and produces the fruit. In reality, a branch doesn't need to do anything but "abide" in the vine to have life and produce fruit. Jesus was trying to impress upon His disciples that when we "abide" in Christ by fully trusting Him, He is free to speak spiritual life into us through His word. This word or spiritual truth allows us to have a spiritual life and produce spiritual results (fruit).

> "Now ye are clean through the word which I have spoken unto you. Abide in me, and I in you. As the branch cannot bear fruit of itself, except it abide in the vine; no more can ye, except ye abide in me. I am the vine. Ye *are* the branches: He that abides in me, and I in him, the same bringeth forth much fruit: for without me ye can do nothing." (Jn 15:3-5)

The third fact that this imaginary hose might know is that it must be attached to some source, such as an open faucet, because it cannot produce its water. It must also rely on an underground pump to supply adequate water to perform as needed. I must emphasize that the hose does not get water from the faucet; it only gets water through it. Let's say that the faucet, in this case, represents the theologies and practices of particular churches. Sadly, many churches are under the impression that it is only through *their* doctrines and religious rituals that one can find spiritual life, and in doing so, they tend to close the faucet to genuine spiritual growth. In Paul's day, the issue was whether spiritual life came through a Gentile church that taught uncircumcision or a Jewish church that taught circumcision. Paul emphasized that religious rituals are not the portal to a great spiritual life, but *faith* in Christ is. Therefore,

Paul instructs the Galatian Church that "in Christ, neither circumcision availed anything, nor uncircumcision; but *faith that works by love*." (Gal 5:6 emphasis mine) I am not saying that rituals and doctrines cannot help us in our faith, but only that they cannot be the objects of our worship or be seen as sufficient on their own, apart from faith. The faucet is not the source of the hose's water; the pump is.

Now, let's turn to the other end of the hose. At this end, we usually affix a nozzle with a trigger device to control water flow to the desired plant or object. This end could represent the "love end" of the hose because love always gives. It is the end where the water exits to give life to a plant or cleans some object that needs cleaning. The hose knows that it *cannot* decide to whom or what it provides water and how much. It has to submit itself to a person to make those decisions. Now, I know what you're thinking. "But I'm not a hose and have a right and responsibility to decide whom I should love." My answer to that is the words of Jesus when He said, "I do nothing of myself, but as the Father has taught Me" (John 8:28). Paul later admonished the Church at Ephesus to "walk in love, as Christ also hath loved us and hath given himself *for us* an offering and a sacrifice *to God* for a sweet-smelling savor" (Eph 5:2 emphasis mine). If we want to live obedient lives characterized by God's love, we must love as God loves, not as we wish to love.

It is challenging to understand that because we are not the source of God's life, we cannot determine who may receive that life and how much they may have. We can only put ourselves in God's hand and let Him decide where He wishes to point us and how much of His life he wants to release through us. We have no right to withhold God's presence and love because we disagree with a person's religious stand or lifestyle. That is for God, and God alone, to decide. That is why Paul says that we must present ourselves *to God* as offerings and sacrifices so that he can sovereignly love through us. That is holiness.

Jonah's story gives us a glaring example of a man who thought *he* should be the one to choose the recipients of God's love. Jonah hated the Ninevites. He would have liked nothing better than to see them scorched, and because of that, he decided that there was no way that he would be God's mouthpiece to save the city of Nineveh. How dare God make him do something he didn't want to do? It took facing death in the belly of a fish to make Jonah change his mind and beg for God's mercy – the same compassion he didn't want God to show to the Ninevites. Even after preaching to the Ninevites, he was angry when they repented and received God's mercy. This story shows how easily we allow our prejudices and hatred to stop us from letting God love people of His choosing through us.

The apostle Peter had the same problem. After he failed to stand with Jesus at His trial and experienced the resulting shame, it's safe to assume that Peter felt like a total failure and just wanted to return to his old way of life as a fisherman (John 21:3). He probably didn't want to risk letting Jesus down again. In Peter's case, it was not hatred that made him run but fear of failure. He didn't want to face the shame again of not *walking* the life he was talking about. In this case, God had to intervene through Jesus, who encountered Peter on the beach after a fruitless night of fishing. He gave Peter something that Peter could not provide for himself after a long night of self-effort—breakfast. Then, he got to the heart of the issue.

Jesus said, "Peter, do you love me more than these fish"? And Peter's response was, "Come on, Lord, you know I love you." "Then feed my sheep." Again, Jesus confronted him with, "Peter, do you love me," and again, Peter responded, "Lord, you know that I love you." "Then feed my lambs," Jesus replied. Finally, after a third time, Peter felt somewhat exasperated and hurt. "Come on, Lord, you know everything. You know I love you." This episode makes me wonder how often Christ must ask us whether we love him before we understand what it means to "love God." As Peter discovered, it means to let God so captivate us that we turn over our lives to Him and let Him sovereignly decide whom we are to love and how we are to love. Christ said it this way:

> "Verily, verily, I say unto thee, When you were young, you girded yourself, and walked where you wished: but when you grow old, you shalt stretch forth your hands,

and another shall gird you, and carry where you not wish. He spoke this signifying by what death he should glorify God. And when he had spoken this, he said unto him, Follow me". (John 21:18-19 MKJV)

The final thing the hose knows is that assuming the pump is working and the faucet is open, the nozzle determines whether or not the water will flow through the hose. Fresh water is allowed to flow into the hose by releasing the water. However, it must first release the old water if it wants fresh water. Failure to release the water will cause the water in the hose to stagnate and absorb the odor of the hose. If left to deteriorate long enough, bacteria in the water can grow and cause the water to become unpalatable and unhealthy to drink.

At the beginning of the chapter, I mentioned that one of the verses God gave me for the night sermon was Gal 5:6; "For in Jesus Christ neither circumcision availeth anything, nor uncircumcision; but faith which worketh by love." I believe he is saying that God's love should be the controlling factor in our lives. Without releasing God's life through love, we will see no need for faith to refill ourselves with fresh (Zoe) life. The Laodicean church in Rev 3 claimed that it was "rich, and increased with goods, and needed nothing." (Rev 3:17). However, God's judgment of that church was that it was more like an old hose full of lukewarm, putrefied water. If one tasted that church's spiritual life, they would only spit it out again because of its foul taste. Only by releasing God's life within us through love can we hope to keep our lives fresh and vibrant through faith.

In the fifty-eighth chapter of Isaiah, we find another story that clearly illustrates this last point. During Isaiah's time in Israel's history, the religious leaders added many rituals and rules to the Levitical law, which did not originate from God but rather from their religious zeal. These additions often twisted and perverted the law's purpose as God had given it, such as the fasting ritual.

Chapter 58 begins with God telling Isaiah to declare their transgression concerning their fasting to the people. This transgression involved changing the fast from once a year, which God had mandated, to twice a week, which the religious leaders commanded. In doing this, they also altered the purpose of the fast. One must ask, "Why would the religious leaders impose one hundred and four fasts per year when God only required one?" The only possible answer is that they were trying to impress God and people with their religious zeal and to control the people's lives more regularly.

> "Yet they seek me daily, and delight to know my ways, as a nation that did righteousness, and forsook not the ordinance of their God: they ask of me the ordinances of justice; they take delight in approaching to God. Wherefore have we fasted, *say they* and thou seest not? *"Wherefore* have we afflicted our soul, and thou takest no knowledge"? (Is 58:2,3)

The truth is that God is not impressed with man's self-imposed zeal, only with his obedience. "Behold, to obey *is* better than sacrifice" (1Sa 15:22) . The prideful human nature of man, desiring to impress God and people, tempts a person to institute his worship rituals rather than conform to God's rituals. Through this voluntary zeal, man tends to redefine the purpose of God's religious observances. Such is the case in this chapter, where God asks the question concerning their exercising of the fast:

> "Is it such a fast that I have chosen? A day for a man to afflict his soul? *Is it* to bow down his head as a bulrush, and to spread sackcloth and ashes *under him?* wilt thou call this a fast, and an acceptable day to the LORD?" (Isa 58:5)

We must realize that the purpose of the fast or affliction of their soul was not to have a "pity party" before God, hoping He would feel sorry for them and answer their prayers. It was to teach them that, for God to rescue and restore humanity, He would have to release His son as representative of His life to serve as atonement for sin. Likewise, if God is going to rescue and restore struggling people through us, we must be willing to release the life of God in us in some very practical ways. For example, if God asks you to restore a hungry person, it may cost you some food or money to feed them. It may cost you the sharing of your home if you restore a homeless person. If you are going to help a person needing clothes, you may have to give him the shirt off your back.

> "Is not this the fast that I have chosen? To lose the bands of wickedness, to undo the heavy burdens, and to let the oppressed go free, and that ye break every yoke? *Is it* not to deal thy bread to the hungry, and that thou bring the poor that are cast out to thy house? when thou seest the naked, that thou cover him; and that thou hide not thyself from thine own flesh?" (Isa 58:6,7)

God is asking that we *allow him* to open our hearts in love for people around us who are struggling and let Him release his grace toward all who need it through us. He cannot fill us with fresh grace until we enable him to do this. It is not God's intent that we should merely be a receptacle of his grace but also a conduit. When this happens, we will experience the power of holiness and a fantastic freshness of life that we have never before envisioned, as elaborated in the following verses:

> "Then shall your light break forth like the dawn, and your healing shall spring up speedily; your righteousness shall go before you; the glory of the LORD shall be your rear guard. Then you shall call, and the LORD will answer; you shall cry, and he will say, 'Here I am... If you pour yourself out for the hungry and satisfy the desire of the afflicted, then shall your light rise in the darkness and your gloom be as the noonday. And the LORD will guide you continually and satisfy your desire in scorched places and make your bones strong; and you shall be like a watered garden, like a spring of water, whose waters do not fail."
>
> (Isa 58:8-11 ESV)

An old hymn published in 1900 perfectly captures the concept of holiness as I have described it in this chapter;

1. How I praise Thee, precious Savior,
   That Thy love laid hold of me;
   Thou hast saved and cleansed and filled me,
   That I might Thy channel be.

2. Just a channel full of blessing,
   To the thirsty hearts around,
   To tell out Thy full salvation,
   All Thy loving message sound.

3. Emptied that Thou shouldest fill me,
   A clean vessel in Thy hand;
   With no pow'r but as Thou givest
   Graciously with each command.

4. Witnessing Thy pow'r to save me,
   Setting free from self and sin;
   Thou who bought me to possess me,
   In Thy fullness, Lord, come in.

5. Jesus, fill now with Thy Spirit
   Hearts that full surrender know,
   That the streams of living water
   From our inner man may flow.

Refrain:

Channels only, blessed Master
But with all thy wonderous power
Flowing through us, thou canst use us
Every day and every hour.[3]

---

[3] Mary E. Maxwell, Public domain

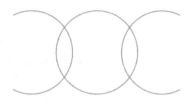

CHAPTER 4

HOLY GROUND

"And he said, draw not nigh hither: put off thy shoes from off thy feet, for the place whereon thou standest *is* holy ground." (Exo 3:5)

"And the captain of the LORD'S host said unto Joshua, loose thy shoe from off thy foot; for the place whereon thou standest *is* holy." (Jos 5:15)

There are two occasions in the Bible where God told men to remove their shoes because they were standing on holy ground. These occur in the stories of Moses and Joshua. It is not immediately clear what made the ground they stood on holy. You may say the ground was holy "because God was there," and I won't argue that point with you. Indeed, any place where the Lord displays Himself could be deemed holy, as in the Tabernacle. However, I believe there is something more significant in these passages that we need to explore.

First, I would like to look at Moses's experience in the Exodus account. Moses was in the Sinai desert, tending his father-in-law's sheep, when he noticed a bush burning. Since this was a dry region, that was no big thing except that, as it burned, the fire did not consume the bush. This phenomenon caught Moses' attention, so he went over to investigate. As he neared the bush, he heard a voice coming from the flaming bush saying, "Don't get too close to the fire and take off your shoes because you're standing on holy ground." The voice then identified itself, saying, "I'm the god of your father, Abraham and Isaac and Jacob." That could strike fear into a man's heart. Moses knew the gods of the Egyptians and maybe those of his father-in-law; however, he had never encountered the God of his forefathers and was terrified. I've wondered if Moses heard about Yahweh from his mother as she cared for him during his early childhood. The NIV says, "I am the God of your father, the God of Abraham, Isaac, and the God of Jacob." He seems to refer to Moses's actual father (Amram) here, not to his "father Abraham."

Then God proceeded to tell Moses that He had a job for him. "Go back to Egypt and talk to the leaders of your people. Get them to go with you to tell Pharaoh to let My people go." Moses asked, "And who should I tell them sent me?" God responds, "I AM THAT I AM; tell them I AM sent you." Can you imagine what was going on in Moses' mind? He is eighty and has been hiding in the desert for forty years because he's on the Egyptian "hit list." Now, God wants him to waltz into the palace of the most powerful man on the planet and tell him to release all his slaves and let them leave the country. Is that all? God continues: Pharaoh will not listen to you at first, but when I get done with the Egyptians, they will beg you to go and pay you off with silver, gold, and any other valuables they can come up with to help you go.

Moses' reaction was typical of how the average Christian today would react to such a command—with excuses. He tells God, "I'm a no-body. I can't speak. They won't listen." We also respond with excuses to God's commands partly because we have a very dysfunctional concept of holiness. To most people, Holiness is some ethereal, religious quality of perfection and purity that we must have to go to heaven. But if we continue to operate with that anemic definition, God will never be able to accomplish great things through us. I use the term anemic because people who define holiness that way tend to see holiness as a passive state of being. "Ok, I'm holy; now what"? They don't see it as a prerequisite for spiritual action. Christ saw His sanctification as a prerequisite to sanctifying His followers. (Joh 17:19) Paul saw holiness as the foundation of all his activities. "I can do all things through Christ which strength-eneth me" (Php 4:13). God is looking for men and women who will stand with Him on the holy ground of complete unity and oneness to do great things.

> "For the eyes of the LORD run to and fro throughout
> the whole earth, to shew himself strong on behalf of
> *them* whose heart *is* perfect toward him...."
>
> (2Ch 6:9)

Major Ian Thomas (1914-2007), a highly regarded Englishman, had a favorite expression that echoes that thought; "God is not concerned about our ability or inability but our availability." I believe God asked Moses to remove his shoes to provoke awe and reverence and keep Moses from running off. Traversing that wild and rugged terrain without shoes would be very hazardous. Like Moses, we tend to draw back or run when God calls us to stand with Him in holiness and see the power He wishes to share with us.

I remember how this occurred in my life many years ago. I minis-tered in my first church for twenty years and planned to spend the rest of my life there. However, a problem arose in the church, and I could not find a solution. The more I tried to solve the problem, the worse it became. Finally, my wife and I decided to get away to reflect and dis-cuss the situation. We took our camper and went to one of our favorite areas in Southern Indiana to camp for a few days. While we were there, I remember walking down a back road, feeling that the weight on my shoulders was pushing me down into the gravel roadway. God finally spoke to me sometime later while painting my neighbor's house. He told me I could let Him handle the problem or choose to earn a living by the sweat of my brow. That was my call to stand on holy ground with God, and I muffed it. Having struggled with this problem for so long, I became very frustrated and relatively short-tempered. Finally, in my frustration, I looked back to heaven and defiantly said, "I'll earn it with the sweat of my brow." A few months later, I walked away from the church God had so miraculously given me and started a construction company. Boy, did I sweat!

For the next twenty-some years, I worked as an assistant pastor at three different churches–two were unpaid part-time positions while I ran my construction company, and one was full-time after I shut my business down. Looking back, I believe that walking away from my first church was the worst decision of my life because I had walked away from a pastorate God had given me. From then on, I felt God would only trust me to work under the leadership of other pastors, which I did. However, now, I realize I was wrong to assume that God gave up on me. I now know I made that assumption out of guilt and shame because I had let God down. Those years were frustrating because I could not speak from my heart. I had to submit to someone else's vision and could not follow the Holy Spirit. I had to agree with the head pastor if I wanted to speak from his pulpit, even if I felt he was sometimes wrong. This condition caused conflict in my relationship with these pastors and ended with me leaving those positions rather than causing strife. Paul states, "The servant of the Lord must not strive" (2 Tim 2:24). Recently, I have realized that I must, once again, seek that holy ground with God where I am free to take my orders from God alone. This may be part of Paul's thought when he said he didn't want to build on another man's foundation. (Rom 15:20)

I am not saying that working under another pastor's ministry is wrong or impossible. Sometimes, it can be constructive, as in the case of Paul and Timothy, where a young minister may need mentoring. However, shared ministries can be complicated, especially when the pastors have different visions. You may think this goes against everything I have discussed in this book, and you would be right to some extent. Ideally, in holiness, we should be able to work as one. The problem is that none of us have arrived yet at that point of complete holiness with God, making it difficult, if not impossible, to walk in holiness with other people. Even Paul and Barnabus had their disagreements and went their separate ways. Paul also writes in his letters that quite a few of his coworkers had left him, some for the world and some for their ministries. He readily admits that he sometimes struggled with the problem of holiness.

"Not as though I had already attained, either were already perfect: but I follow after, if that I may apprehend that for which also I am apprehended of Christ Jesus. Brethren, I count not myself to have apprehended: but *this* one thing *I do,* forgetting those things which are behind, and reaching forth unto those things which are before, I press toward the mark for the prize of the high calling of God in Christ Jesus. Let us, therefore, as many as be perfect, be thus minded: and if in anything ye be otherwise minded, God shall reveal even this unto you. Nevertheless, whereto we have already attained, let us walk by the same rule; let us mind the same thing." (Php 3:12-16) (emphasis mine)

Since then, I've realized I must seek God's unique ministry. I am happy that God has again entrusted me with a ministry that I call "my church without walls." It is not a church per se, but God seems to send people struggling with some significant problems into my life. Some of them have come from 30-40 miles away. I also enjoy conversing with old and new friends while eating breakfast at the Speedway café or McDonald's. He has also sent me to pastor older adults in my community who have lost loved ones or are struggling in their later years. So once again, I am watching God do through me what He desires and can only echo the words of Dr. Helen Schucman when she writes:

> "I am here only to be truly helpful.
> I am here to represent Him Who sent me.
> I do not have to worry about what to say or what to do
>   because He Who sent me will direct me.
> I am content to be wherever He wishes, knowing He goes
>   there with me.
> I will be healed as I let Him teach me to heal".[4]

---

[4] Schucman, Dr. Helen. A Course in Miracles (p. 26). Foundation for Inner Peace. Kindle Edition.

In the second occurrence of God asking a man to remove his shoes because he was standing on holy ground, we find Joshua coming to grips with God's call to holiness. Joshua was Moses' protégé and loyal go-to guy in the wilderness. When Moses lost his temper with the people and was banned by God from entering the promised land, God put Joshua in charge and commanded him to bring the Israelites into Canaan. (Jos 1:2) I'm sure that Joshua felt highly overwhelmed. However, God reassured Joshua that He would be with him as He was with Moses and promised Joshua success in his mission to claim the land for Israel. God then admonished him three times to be strong and of good courage.

Joshua made no excuses as Moses did when called to God's mission. He immediately took charge and brought the Israelites across the Jordon River to Gilgal on the plains of Jericho. There, he had them build a memorial of twelve stones taken from the Jordon to remind future generations of what God had done there. Joshua also obeyed God and circumcised all the men born in the wilderness. Then, they celebrated their first Passover in the land God gave them. Finally, God stopped the manna he had supplied for them for the last Forty years and told them they could now eat the land's fruit. In short, God confirmed to Israel that He was a Holy God who had stood by them and kept His promise. He had delivered them from the reproach of their old life in Egypt and brought them to the new life He had promised. The Children of Israel could now move forward and occupy the land on the strength of that fulfilled promise.

The Bible does not say how long the Israelites stayed at Gilgal, but Joshua took walks out on the plain while they were there and viewed his first obstacle–the walled city of Jericho. I'm sure he was going over some possible strategies to overtake the city in his mind. Then, one day, as he contemplated, he saw a man confronting him with a drawn sword. Somewhat astonished, Joshua asked the stranger a critical question; "Art thou for us, or our adversaries?" to which the stranger responded, "No, but as captain of the host of the Lord, I now come." (Jos 5: 13,14) In other words, I'm not here primarily to meet your or their needs but

God's. Then the man told Joshua to remove his shoes because he was standing on holy ground. (vs.15)

Now, as we compare the stories of Moses and Joshua, we find several similarities.

1. In both experiences, each man was approximately eighty years old.
2. They were both asked to be a part of something beyond their abilities.
3. Both men had just spent forty years in the desert, a place of bareness and hardship when God told them that he would do something great through them.
4. In each case, God asked each man to remove his shoes because he was standing on holy ground.
5. Each man ultimately submitted to God's authority and power.

In the case of Joshua, however, I believe the ultimate purpose of holiness is more fully exposed. That purpose is, first, to meet God's needs. Often, if not always, we tend to enter into prayer with the idea of having our own immediate needs met. This is not wrong. God tells us to ask. James states, "We have not because we ask not" (James 4:2). However, It is seldom our first instinct to give thought to the needs of God.

In the Lord's prayer, Christ prefaced His prayer by praying, "Thy kingdom come; Thy will be done on earth as it is in heaven." To Him, His father's need came first. If this is a model for us to follow, we must also be mindful that God's needs must come first. The desire expressed in that prayer was the reason Jesus, in holiness, went to the cross. The writer of Hebrews states, "who for the joy (of the kingdom) that was set before Him, endured the cross, despising the shame, and is set down at the right hand of the throne of God (in His kingdom)." (Heb 12:2) (emphasis mine)

In an earlier chapter, I mentioned that holiness is a two-way street. We do not stand on holy ground with God solely to have our needs met but to fulfill the needs and desires of God. Holy ground is where God meets us and calls us to collaborate to redeem His people. God called

Moses and Joshua to stand in holiness with Him, not just to free the
Jews from slavery and bring them into Canaan, where their lives could be
more fulfilling. He called them because He had chosen the Jewish people
to be the people through which He would reestablish His kingdom rule
on the earth. We also must look beyond the immediate situation in our
holy union with Christ and realize God is calling us to do something
for Him that we cannot do in our power. When we consent in holiness
to glorify God by meeting His need, He, in turn, will celebrate us by
attending to *our* needs.

"I will glorify the house of my glory" (Is 60:7).

"Delight thyself also in the LORD, and he shall give
thee the desires of thine heart" (Psa 37:4).

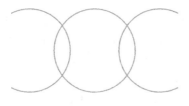

CHAPTER 5

HOLINESS AS REFLECTED IN THE HUMAN BODY

Before I begin this section, I must clarify that I am not equating nature or the universe with God when discussing holiness in the physical world, as does pantheism or Spinozism. In some form, these metaphysical philosophies equate God to nature rather than acknowledging Him as the deity who created nature. I am not saying my body is God because it operates in holiness but reflects a creator who works in perfect holiness. Paul states that God's invisible nature can be understood through the things He created in the same way that Picasso's paintings reflect his mind.

> "For the invisible things of him from the creation of the world are clearly seen, being understood by the things that are made, *even* His eternal power and Godhead; so that they are without excuse." (Rom 1:20)

Therefore, when we see a living organism such as the human body demonstrating a great sense of unity or holiness in its functioning, we can assume its creator is holy.

The Bible describes three organisms as bodies: the human body, the marriage body, and the church body. However, many different forms of body life exist in the physical world. Each species is unique and one of a kind in form. However, they all have three things in common: they are life-sustaining, capable of growth, and capable of reproduction.

All inorganic matter, such as rock, water, and air, is governed by immutable physical laws that mathematical and chemical formulas can describe. However, living organisms have a quality we call "life" and are *doing* something rather than just *being* something. They all contain many parts that function in complete harmony, thus allowing them to maintain life, grow, and procreate.

In the case of the human body, David proclaimed, "I will praise thee; for I am fearfully *and* wonderfully made" (Psa 139:14). Medical and psychological sciences are beginning to discover the extreme complexities of the human body and mind. It is impressive that, in an average, healthy person, approximately 50 trillion cells work together to maintain life functions. Each of these cells appears to have a brain that processes information from its environment. This cellular brain is not located in the cell's nucleus as once thought but in the cell's outer membrane. It controls what enters and exits the cell as well as the functions of the cell. Also, scientists have found that genetics do not exclusively determine the cell's operation but that our beliefs and values can also highly influence the nature and function of the cell.

So, the question may arise, "How do these 50 trillion little cell brains work together for the common good of the corporate body?" The human brain coordinates all cellular interactions through two methods: the nervous system and the endocrine or hormonal system. These systems regulate body processes through chemical and electrical signals that pass between cells to integrate, coordinate, and respond to sensory information the body receives from its surroundings.

In the nervous system, the brain receives and sends messages electrochemically through the body, employing chemicals that cause an electrical impulse from one cell to another. When the brain receives impulses from the body, it instantly interprets them according to the mind's program. It then sends impulses targeting specific organs and tissues of the body through passages called meridians, instructing them on how to behave. Because this system is electrical, it moves extremely fast and is short-lived. On the other hand, the endocrine system is set in motion when an electrical impulse is sent to a gland or organ, telling it to secrete a specific hormone. These hormones are secreted into the bloodstream to target organs, affecting a more widespread and sustained response.

This description of communication in the body is grossly oversimplified; however, one should see that if this system of information transfer breaks down through something such as MS or Alzheimer's, the body becomes disabled or dies. Therefore, the *relationship* of parts may be more critical to the body's survival than a particular part's performance. This relational unity of the body pictures what I call "holiness."

One may ask, "What determines how the brain instructs the body to behave?" The brain is a very sophisticated computer that processes information based on programs we collectively call the mind. The brain is the hardware, and the mind is the software. Therefore, the mind is the sole determiner of how the brain coordinates the body's behavior. Both scripture and science agree on this.

"And be renewed in the spirit of your mind;" (Eph 4:23)

"And be not conformed to this world: but be ye transformed by the renewing of your mind..." (Rom 12:2)

"Research by Princeton University showed that self-fulfilling prophecy is just that, and what we actively believe tends to manifest in our behavior and that of others. This is what they call a "creative social reality," a serious issue that affects everything from stock prices to the arms race, not to mention everyday interactions (and, additionally, the details of one's personal health)."[5]

Next, we must ask, "Who or what determines the programs in the mind and assures us that the mind's program will effectively maintain

---

[5] Hawkins, David R. Healing and Recovery (p. 30). Veritas Publishing. Kindle Edition.

a healthy body unification?" Every program needs a programmer. At this level, we must consider the spiritual realm of life, which is infinite and non-linear. In the medical world, much disagreement exists about the nature or reality of the spiritual realm and its effect on our body's health. Most medical professionals still claim that all mental programs come through our five senses and depend solely on sensory input from the world about us. If true, we must conclude that humans are pawns of their environment, and health solutions are possible only from chemical and biological sources. However, since the turn of the century, some scientists have concluded there is a connection between our spiritual beliefs and physical well-being. For example, Bruce Lipton, a cellular biologist and teacher in medical schools, has written a book called "The Biology of Belief." In this book, he states,

> "The fact that scientific principles led me, a nonseeker, to spiritual insight is appropriate because the latest discoveries in physics and cell research are forging new links between the worlds of Science and Spirit."[6]

Christians accept that there is a side of us we call our flesh nature, or ego, which acquires its programming through the five senses. Paul describes this process as being "conformed to this world" (Rom 12:2). However, we also hold that we are a spirit created by a divine being (God) for fellowship. When we reconcile ourselves to fellowship with God (holiness) through His redemptive plan, we can receive programming from God that will far surpass the quality of programming we get from our environment and which, according to Paul, will transform our lives. Godly programming will more effectively maintain that sense of oneness or holiness in our bodies and produce health.

It is not by chance that the Bible uses the imagery of the human body to explain the workings and interactions of the marriage and church bodies. Although there are no perfect parallels between the three bodies,

---

[6] Lipton, Bruce H. The Biology of Belief 10th Anniversary Edition (p. 203). Hay House. Kindle Edition.

we can make many comparisons. Lipton compares the holiness of the human body to life in general when he states:

> "Imagine a population of trillions of individuals living under one roof in a state of perpetual happiness. Such a community exists—it is called the healthy human body. Clearly, cellular communities work better than human communities—there are no left-out, "homeless" cells in our bodies."[7]

* * *

In my discussion of "body holiness," my primary focus will be on the head's role and function in its relationship to the body. The body has no awareness of itself. For example, the arms cannot think and, therefore, have no understanding that they are arms. The same is true of every other body part–even cells with a brain but no self-awareness. Because of this lack of awareness of itself, it is not in the body that we experience life. Our senses are experienced only in the mind at a level we call consciousness. There is no body awareness when there is a loss of consciousness, as when we are under anesthesia.

Because all body consciousness takes place in the mind, two facts emerge. First, the body cannot coordinate itself and must submit itself to the leadership of the head. Secondly, the head must accept responsibility for the welfare of the body by coordinating and facilitating its interactions with the outside world. This head-body, or mind-body relationship, determines how well the body survives and operates appropriately. In terms of holiness, we must say that the condition of holiness, or unity, within the body cannot exist unless there is a perfect union of the head and body. If the head does not maintain a proper or "holy" relationship with the body, neither can function correctly. In the following two chapters, I will explore this head-body connection as it manifests in marriage and church bodies.

---

[7] Ibid (pg. 216)

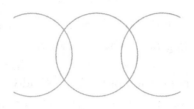

CHAPTER 6

HOLINESS AS REFLECTED IN THE MARRIAGE BODY

When couples come to me wanting to get married, I will usually bait them with the following questions:

> Me: Why do you want to get married?
> Their usual response: We love each other.
> Me: What do you mean by that?
> Their typical response: (Confused stares at each other).

Romantic love seems to be that unexplainable attraction to someone, which is usually somewhat self-serving. I am not saying that is wrong, for one of the benefits of a holy relationship is that both parties gain something they desire and need. God tells us that He wants to give us the desires of our hearts. However, few people enter marriage clearly, understanding their spouse's needs and shortcomings. They, therefore, fail to see marriage as a relationship where they will need to give to the relationship as well as get. Marriage is not a relationship in which you live happily ever after but a relationship in which you must be willing to change if you want it to succeed. One of my favorite sayings is, "If you don't want to change, don't get married." I could also add, "If you don't want to change, don't seek a holy relationship with God." I will speak on these later in this chapter. The goal to be pursued in marriage must be holiness. We must seek to be one body working together as the human body discussed in the last chapter. Couples are destined for a rough road or divorce when this does not happen.

Although the term "marriage body" is not found in the Bible, we see marriage described by "one flesh" in several places, such as in the Genesis scripture below and again in the fifth chapter of Ephesians. Throughout human history, marriage has taken some very different forms and characteristics. I will not take the time to evaluate these. Instead, I aim to look closely at the biblical idea of marriage and how it reflects God's holiness. In examining that Biblical model, I will explore the concepts of submission, authority, sanctification, and healing.

In the book of Genesis, we find the first mention of the terms "husband" and "wife."

> "And the rib, which the LORD God had taken from man, made he a woman and brought her unto the man. (vs.22) And Adam said, this *is* now bone of my bones, and flesh of my flesh: she shall be called woman because she was taken out of Man (vs.23). Therefore shall a man leave his father and his mother, and shall cleave unto his wife: and they shall be one flesh." (Gen 2:22-24 emphasis mine)

This passage indicates that the male-female relationship in marriage is not the same as that of men and women outside of marriage. In verses 22 and 23, the words "man" and "Adam" are translated from the Hebrew word "adam" (aw-dawm'), which means "humanity" or "human being." However, in the rest of that passage, the term "man" is translated from the Hebrew word "iysh" (eesh), meaning "husband." When the Bible speaks of the husband being the head of the wife, it does not use the word "aw-dawm," which refers to all men, but only the word "iysh." Although there is some variance in the use of these terms in different contexts, I take my cue from the second chapter of Hosea, where God speaks of Israel as an unfaithful wife. Here, God says He will return Israel to

Himself by proving to her that He is her husband (iysh) and not her boss (baali). I will look at this passage in more depth later in this chapter.

The Bible makes no distinctions between men's and women's roles outside marriage because we are all "Adam" or human beings. As Galatians 3:28 says, "There is neither Jew nor Greek (ethnic differences), there is neither bond nor free (social differences), there is neither male nor female (sexual differences), for ye are all one in Christ Jesus" (additions mine). Elsewhere in the Bible, we see that Deborah, the wife of Lapidoth, ruled over Israel as a judge (Judges 4:4). The virtuous woman described in Proverbs 31 was a faithful wife and a multifaceted businesswoman. Lydia, a lady of Thyatira, is mentioned in Acts *only* as a businesswoman—a seller of purple.

While Paul did recommend a relatively passive role for women in the Church, I would suggest that he did so primarily out of respect for cultural norms of the time relating to husbands and wives. There were, however, many women he commended highly for their service to the Church. In Rome, Priscilla and her husband were his fellow workers, hosting a church in their home, risking their lives for him (Rom 16:3-5). He also mentions Mary, Tryphea, Tryphosa, Persis, the mother of Rufus, Julia, and others who worked extremely hard with him (Rom 16:6-16). In Philippi, there were Euodia and Syntyche who, though they argued a lot, labored and struggled with Paul in the gospel (Phil 4:2-3). Paul also praises the "unfeigned faith" of Lois and Eunice, the grandmother and mother of Timothy, who taught Timothy to trust God (II Tim 1:5). He also tells us that Lydia of Thyatira exercised great hospitality toward himself and Silas when they left prison. This list is not exhaustive, but it shows that Paul highly regarded women who served the Church.

In his instructions regarding women's behavior in the Church, Paul seemed concerned that peripheral issues would not become the Church's primary focus, thus distracting from the gospel's central theme. He explains this attitude when he writes:

> "And unto the Jews, I became as a Jew, that I might gain
> the Jews; to them that are under the law, as under the law,

that I might gain them that are under the law; to them that are without law, as without law, (being not without law to God, but under the law to Christ,) that I might gain them that are without law. To the weak became I as weak, that I might gain the weak: I am made all things to all *men,* that I might, by all means, save some. *And this I do for the gospel's sake,* that I might be partaker thereof with *you.*" (I Cor 9:20-23 emphasis mine)

It was for the same reason that Paul had his young protégé Timothy – a Gentile – circumcised when he accompanied Paul to Jerusalem, even though Paul strongly opposed physical circumcision as a criterion for being a follower of Christ.

When we turn our attention to the marriage union, the Bible teaches that there are different roles for husbands and wives, though neither is deemed superior to the other. To see the husband's role as inherently superior to the wife's is a cultural prejudice that has been placed upon the Biblical text. Men who try to dominate and diminish their wives are not behaving in a godly manner and will not produce a holy marriage. Instead, they are more likely to create a highly dysfunctional "union."

In his Ephesian letter, Paul compares the husband-wife relationship to Christ and the Church. In this context, he teaches married couples what they should focus on in their marriage.

"Submitting yourselves one to another in the fear of God. Wives, submit yourselves unto your own husbands, as unto the Lord. For the husband is the head of the wife, even as Christ is the head of the Church: and he is the saviour of the body. Therefore as the Church is subject unto Christ, so *let* the wives *be* to their own husbands in everything. Husbands, love your wives, even as Christ also loved the Church, and gave himself for it; that he might sanctify and cleanse it with the washing of water by the word, that he might present it to himself a glorious church, not having spot, or wrinkle,

or any such thing; but that it should be holy and without
blemish. So ought men to love their wives as their own
bodies. He that loveth his wife loveth himself. For no
man ever yet hated his own flesh; but nourisheth and
cherisheth it, even as the Lord the Church: For we are
members of his body, of his flesh, and of his bones. For
this cause shall a man leave his father and mother and
shall be joined unto his wife, and they two shall be one
flesh." (Eph 5:21-31)

The first thing to be noticed in this passage is that Paul prefaces his
discussion of the marriage relationship by saying that, out of respect for
God, all human beings must submit to each other (vs. 21). I take this to
mean that we are all creations made in the image of God and, therefore,
must regard each other equally with dignity and respect. This attitude
also applies to the marriage relationship. A discussion I once had with
my widowed mother brought this to my attention, compelling and personal. A few years after my father died, my mother and I were having a
casual conversation when, out of the blue, she said something I've never
forgotten. She said, "Your father never treated me as an equal. He always
treated me as a teenage girl." Growing up, I had never noticed that. I
thought their marriage was typical. So, when I got married, I treated
my wife the same way and thought nothing of it. This revelation from
my mother became one of my life's significant "grow up" moments. It
took time to root out that engrained attitude I learned from my father.

So, the question becomes: how does this mutual submission work
out in marriage when Paul says the man is the head of the wife as Christ
is the head of the Church? Because the man has authority, is he considered superior to the wife? My answer is a definite "NO." Authority does
not equal superiority! To explain this, we must examine Christ's mindset
concerning the Church.

"Let this mind be in you, which was also in Christ Jesus:
Who, being in the form of God, thought it not robbery
to be equal with God: But made himself of no reputation,

and took upon him the form of a servant, and was made in the likeness of men: And being found in fashion as a man, he humbled himself, and became obedient unto death, even the death of the cross." (Php 2:5-8)

Following Christ's example, we can see the attitude we must have when God gives us authority. Our first reaction must be to accept that authority but walk it out as God ordained–through servanthood. When we flaunt our authority, we lose it. Based on the above scripture, Paul outlines five steps we must take for God to validate that authority in the eyes of those we lead.

1. We must lay aside our self-image as "the boss."
2. We must assume the mindset of a servant.
3. We must identify with those we serve. Learn to listen.
4. We must humble ourselves.
5. We must be willing to die to ourselves for those we lead.

I see this as the proper submission of leaders, and I can tell you from experience that it works. I have seen it work in my marriage and my roles as principal and pastor.

If I could summarize the goal of a husband's leadership role in a marriage, it would be that he must see himself as the savior and life-giver of the marriage body (Eph 5:23). This leadership goal in marriage is no different than good leadership in general. For instance, a sports team's success will never exceed the coach's supervision. The success of any business or corporation will never exceed the management skills of the owner or CEO. Virtually all organizational research verifies that as the head goes, so goes the body.

Paul is not implying in his discussion that a wife is less important than her husband, only that her form of submission differs from that of her husband. Her submission is to respect and connect to her husband's leadership (vs. 22). Paul does not say she should function as a doormat or a submissive little puppy. God has endowed her with the skills and abilities to carry out the duties required in running a home and working outside the home, about which husbands can only dream. If a husband is wise, he will (1) respect her for that, (2) encourage her to express her viewpoint, and (3) listen to her–really listen to her. Again, this is not only true about good leadership in the home. It is valid in all good leadership. When, as a principal, I began to listen to my teachers and respect their viewpoints, running the school got a lot easier.

As Paul concludes his discussion of holiness (one flesh) in marriage in Ephesians 5, he makes an almost comical statement at the end when he says, "This is a great mystery" (Eph 5:32a). Does Paul understand the depths of what is meant by "marriage"? Probably not. But he concludes, "Nevertheless let every one of you in particular so love his wife even as himself, and the wife *see* that she reverence *her* husband" (Eph 5:33). In other words, he is saying that we cannot merely follow our egotistical understanding of authority for holiness to work in marriage. To the ego, holiness is impossible. The ego cannot comprehend holiness. True holiness in marriage is attainable only as both husband and wife exercise their love for each other by submitting, at the outset, to the authority and guidance of the Holy Spirit. Paul emphasizes this firmly at the beginning of Ephesians 5.

> "And walk in love, as Christ also hath loved us, and hath
> given himself for us an offering and a sacrifice to God
> for a sweet-smelling savor." (Eph 5:2)

And interestingly enough, he repeats that admonishment to husbands in the twenty-fifth verse. So, maybe he is implying that good leadership initiates good behavior.

So, how do husbands and wives sanctify (set apart) their mate to themselves, producing holiness in their marriage? Indeed, they consecrate themselves to each other at the wedding; however, they must walk it out daily to experience the reality of that sanctification. They do not just live happily ever after—that's fairy tale stuff.

To sanctify a spouse is to set them apart from everyone else in a relationship of complete unity or holiness. Holiness, however, requires mutual sanctification. Therefore, you must first sanctify (set apart) yourself to that person before you can sanctify them to yourself. Like love, sanctification is not something you bring about by force but by attraction. Therefore, we must follow the example of Christ in both love and sanctification.

"We love Him because he first loved us." (I Jn 4:19)

"...I (Christ) sanctify myself that they also might be sanctified..." (John 17:19, emphasis mine)

To better understand how a husband achieves a wife's sanctification, we must go to Hos 2:14-15. Here, we see God telling Hosea the five steps He will use to sanctify and attract Israel into a holy relationship with Him. They are as follows:

1. "I will allure her." (vs. 14) The husband's first responsibility is to make himself attractive—spiritually, intellectually, emotionally, and physically. A man once came to me complaining that his wife left him for another man and wanted to know how to get her back. My answer was simple. "Be a better man than he is." I think it is time that we men "man up" and become the leaders God wants us to be—attractive, not forceful!

2. "Bring her into the wilderness." (vs. 14) Our second responsibility is to create times when we take our wives away from the rat race of life and spend time listening to them. These are the times when we make her feel that she is not just part of our world but, as far as the marriage is concerned, that she *is* our world. We must cherish her.

3. "Speak comfortably unto her." (vs. 14) An old saying says, "Communication is the lifeblood of a marriage." The root word of communication is to commune, which means sharing or having everything in common. In this phrase, the keyword is "comfortably," which means that the husband should not out-debate his wife to establish dominance but should listen to her and make her feel safe to share her heart's deep hurts and secrets.

4. <u>"Give her her vineyards"</u> (vs. 15). Vineyards represent areas in a woman's life where she can develop her life creatively and enjoy the fruits of her labor. Husbands must not hinder their wives from developing their gifts since these make their wives unique; they give them an identity beyond being wives.

5. <u>"and the valley of Achor for a door of hope"</u> (vs. 15). Achor means "trouble" or "affliction" and implies a severe kind of trouble. During these times, husbands must provide their wives with a door of hope. To be a man who instills hope is probably the most challenging goal a husband can achieve. He must have great courage to face difficulties without sidestepping issues and casting blame. It will require that he be highly disciplined in the spiritual qualities of love, joy, peace, longsuffering, gentleness, goodness, faith, meekness, and self-control. If he does not develop these qualities, he may bail on his leadership responsibility in tough times, forcing his wife to cope with the problem and losing her trust and respect.

As the head, the husband must assume leadership responsibility to establish holiness or unity in the marriage, allowing the wife to thrive and grow. However, this is not to say that women cannot initiate their husbands' sanctification. On the contrary, Paul states that a wife can significantly impact her husband's consecration to herself and God.

"For the unbelieving husband is sanctified by the wife,
and the unbelieving wife is sanctified by the husband:
else were your children unclean, but now are they holy."
(1Co 7:14)

Peter also says that a woman can affect her husband's sanctification to God and herself by how she conducts herself (I Pet 3:1-4). I believe that women can affect their husbands' change through an attitude of respect. I agree with Peter that it is not so much the outer beauty that affects a man's sanctification but her inner beauty– the beauty of a gentle and quiet spirit and her loyalty to him.

Once a couple has established a relationship of holiness in their marriage, they can begin to address their faults (vs. 26). But before I address this topic, I would like to repeat the two statements I made earlier: (1) If you don't want to change, don't get married, and (2) If you don't want to change, don't seek God. As harsh as those statements may seem, both relationships will demand change in our lives if they are to work. Holy relationships are the most powerful change agents in life. These relationships will not only require a change in your behavior but will empower change through mutual love, faith, and encouragement. The Apostle John makes this point in his first letter to the Church. Regarding our relationship with God, He states:

> "If we say that we have fellowship (holiness) with him, and walk in darkness, we lie, and do not the truth: But if we walk in the light (truth), as he is in the light, we have fellowship (holiness) one with another, and the blood of Jesus Christ his Son cleanseth us from all sin… If we confess our sins, he is faithful and just to forgive us *our* sins and to cleanse us from all unrighteousness." (I Jn 1:6,7,9 emphasis mine)

Paul says that when we pursue true holiness or fellowship with God, that holiness will always create righteousness in our lives. Because holiness and righteousness are so closely intertwined, many people equate them. However, I believe they are two different spiritual qualities. Holiness is relational, while righteousness is behavioral.

In marriage, cleansing does not mean that a spouse (thinking they are perfect) corrects their spouse. No, that will only cause a war! Feeling a constant need to "correct" someone is more of an expression of pride than love. Trying to fix people through judgmentalism and coercion can only address overt behavior, not the underlying source of that behavior, which is the brokenness of their hearts. Spiritual cleansing is more about healing the heart than correcting behavior. That is why Jesus stated that his purpose for coming to this earth was to heal the brokenhearted and preach deliverance, recovery, and freedom (Lk 4:18). He did not come to add or enforce more rules. In the same spirit, husbands and wives must first own up to their flaws and imperfections. Then, with a heart of love and holiness, they can forgive their also-imperfect spouse and give them the love and support needed to heal and cleanse. I believe James sums this up exceptionally well when he writes:

> "Confess *your* faults one to another, and pray one for another, that ye may be healed. The effectual fervent prayer of a righteous man availeth much." (Jas 5:16)

I end this discussion by stating that there is a cost associated with sanctification, both in marriage and in our relationship with God. Yes, Christ has paid the price of our justification. However, there is a price we must be willing to pay to attain holiness. In marriage, God gave us an arena to understand and work out the spiritual mysteries of holiness and righteousness. When marriage is viewed only as a means to satisfy our egotistical needs, its real purpose is lost. In like manner, coming to Jesus only to be freed from hell or get rich misses salvation's real purpose. The true purpose of marriage and salvation is to bring people into holiness. "Follow peace with all *men*, and holiness, without which no man shall see the Lord" (Heb 12:14).

Jesus taught there was a high cost in following Him and that many who fail to consider that cost will give up and be scorned by those who are watching.

> "For which of you, intending to build a tower, sitteth not down first, and counteth the cost, whether he have *sufficient* to finish *it?* Lest haply, after he hath laid the foundation, and is not able to finish *it,* all that behold *it* begin to mock him, saying, This man began to build, and was unable to finish." (Luk 14:28-30)

The foundation of marriage is the wedding, where a couple pledges themselves to each other. Couples spend exorbitant sums of money on that wedding. However, they fail to see that the cost of having a good marriage far exceeds the cost of the wedding. The divorce rates of both Christian and non-Christian marriages are close to 50% simply because couples do not consider the actual cost of being married before taking that step. That cost involves allowing holiness to be so valued in their marriage that it transforms who they are.

The same is true in our relationship with God. In Christianity, the foundation of salvation is when we accept Christ as our savior and commit ourselves to Him. Christ has paid an enormous price to make that commitment possible. However, if the Church explains that commitment is only a way to get out of hell, we have gravely misled the new believer. Jesus says that there is a cost that we must consider in following Him. It is the cost of giving up our self-righteousness, which is a disguise for pride. It is also the cost of giving up the sins we enjoy and our judgment and hatred of those who sin differently than we do. We must also consider the loss of the world's favor. The cost of holiness demands that we live as one with God–I in God and God in me. We have been dishonest when we do not tell new Christians the cost and purpose of living the Christian life. As a result, many contemporary Christians enthusiastically start their walk with God but give up on God when facing trials. However, I must say that holiness in marriage and salvation is well worth the price we must pay.

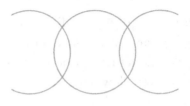

CHAPTER 7

HOLINESS IN THE CHURCH

As I move from the marriage body to an analysis of the church body, I want to state that the human body and the marriage body are physical reflections of our holy relationship with God. They are "shadows" of spiritual truth, as are some Old Testament rules and traditions.

> "Let no man, therefore, judge you in meat, or in drink, or in respect of a holy day, or of the new moon, or of the sabbath *days:* Which are a shadow of things to come; but the body (church) *is* of Christ." (Col 2:16-17 emphasis mine)

Before discussing the church body, I would like to recap the similarities between the marriage and church bodies, as found in Ephesians 5: 21-31.

1. The husband is the head of the marriage body; Christ is the church body's head.
2. As the wife submits to her husband's leadership, so does the Church submit to the administration of Christ.
3. As the husband is the wife's savior, Christ is the Church's savior.
4. As the husband loves his wife by giving himself *to* God *for* her, Christ loves the Church and gives himself to God for it(Eph 5:2).

5. As a husband sanctifies and cleanses (heals) his wife according to biblical principles, not cultural principles, Christ sanctifies and cleanses (restores) the Church according to the principles God laid down to Hosea. (Hos 2)
6. As a husband makes holiness and the well-being of his wife the goal of his marriage, Christ's goal is to present a holy church without blemish to himself.
7. As a husband dedicates himself to making his wife feel special and giving her what she needs to be complete, Christ demonstrates His love for the Church by cherishing and nourishing it.
8. A husband loves his wife as his own body, so Christ loves the Church as Himself.

Paul uses the marriage body's mysterious nature to illustrate Christ's holy relationship with His Church. "This is a great mystery: but I speak concerning Christ and the church" (Eph 5:32) . When I was teaching science, I would always send my students to the lab so that, through a "hands-on" approach, they could more readily grasp and affirm the concepts of my lecture. In the same way, Paul says that when we commit to a "hands-on" working out of the mystery of holiness within the marriage body, we can better comprehend the beauty and purity of Christ's relationship to the Church.

Like the other two bodies, the church body must have a head whose purpose is to coordinate, sanctify, cleanse, and empower it to thrive, thus enabling it to impact the world. Therefore, God has proclaimed Christ the head of the church body.

> "And (God) hath put all *things* under his feet, and gave him *to be* the head over all *things* to the church, which is his body, the fullness of him that filleth all in all." (Eph 1:21-23 emphasis mine)

There are two truths summarized in this scripture. The first is that God has exalted Christ to authority over all creation for all time (Eph 1:20-21). Secondly, God established Christ as head of the Church, making Him one with the Church. These verses imply that God desires to manifest Christ's authority on earth through a holy relationship with His body, the Church.

Yes, we *are* under His authority; however, it is not a master-slave relationship but a husband-wife relationship, as explained in Hosea, chapter two, and Ephesians, chapter five. It resembles Christ's relationship with the Father when He walked this earth. He did not walk this earth as God but as a man indwelt by God in holiness—the same as you and I (Php 2:6, 7).

The writer of Hebrews states that without holiness, no man will see God (Heb 12:14). This verse could have several meanings. First, it could mean that we will not have a vital awareness of God in our lives without holiness. Christ described this awareness when He declared that He and the Father were one (Joh 10:30). Secondly, it could mean that others will not see God in us. Holiness allowed Christ to tell Philip that if he had seen Him, he had seen the Father (John 14:9). Thirdly, it could mean that holiness—oneness with God— is the criteria for heaven. Jesus stated in Matthew 7 and Matthew 25 that at the final judgment, He would reject many who mistakenly assumed they were His followers but did not walk in holiness with Him here on earth. Holiness validated and empowered Christ's ministry on this earth, and holiness confirms and enables the Church to manifest Christ's authority.

In Isaiah's book, the prophet laments that, though God was committed to Israel in holiness, Israel had defiled their holy relationship with God by worshiping false gods and showing disrespect for the poor and needy. Furthermore, although they were still very religious, they took their orders from corrupt political leaders rather than God.

> "To what purpose *is* the multitude of your sacrifices unto me? saith the LORD: I am full of the burnt offerings of rams, and the fat of fed beasts; and I delight not in the blood of bullocks, or of lambs, or of he-goats....How is the faithful city become a harlot! It was full of judgment; righteousness lodged in it, but now

murderers. Thy silver is become dross, thy wine mixed
with water: Thy princes *are* rebellious, and companions
of thieves: everyone loveth gifts, and followeth after
rewards: they judge not the fatherless, neither doth the
cause of the widow come unto them" (Isa 1:11,21-23).

Once, one of my students came to me in the school cafeteria and
said, "I just committed adultery." I replied, "Oh! How so?" His reply
astounded me. "I just added some water to my milk." Wow, I thought.
I had never heard such a profoundly simple description of adultery.
Adultery is the contamination of a pure substance by adding a foreign
substance. In relationships, it degrades a virgin or holy connection with
a competing relationship. This contamination is what Isaiah is talking
about when he says: "Thy silver has become dross, thy wine mixed with
water."

Though the Christian Church has all-too-readily judged Israel's
adulterous behavior as despicable, it has often followed the same adulterous road. The first three hundred years of the Church were years
of great persecution and suffering. They were also the most dynamic
years of the Church regarding spiritual power and God's kingdom's
growth. At the beginning of the fourth century AD, the Roman emperor Constantine supposedly converted to Christianity and declared
Christianity the Roman Empire's state religion. Scholars have debated
his motives since he didn't get baptized until he was on his deathbed.
According to Hans Pohlsander, Professor Emeritus of History at the
University of Albany, State University of New York, Constantine's con-
version was an instrument of politics meant to serve his political interest
in keeping the Empire united under his control.[8] The Church's actions
were no longer the result of a holy relationship with God but were now
serving a political end—the preservation and continuation of the Empire.
This adulterous church-state relationship was passed on to the Roman
Catholic Church and the national churches of Europe and is alive and

---

[8] Pohlsander, The Emperor Constantine, 2nd edition Pages 22-31

well in the United States, where we supposedly adhere to Church and state separation.

Today, the Church is attempting to build God's kingdom through political power and dominance rather than by sacrificial love and service to God for humanity (Eph 5:2, Rom 12:1). In doing so, it has bedded down with some unsavory political leaders and militant organizations. I was deeply pained to see participants in the riotous assault on the US Capital in January of 2021 touting flags with Christian symbols. I believe it significantly damaged the Church's mission and image worldwide.

How many foreign missionaries from the United States labor on the field under the perception that they are trying to "Americanize" people rather than building God's kingdom? Sadly, many American missionaries are unconsciously doing precisely that. Christ declared that He and He alone would build His Church (Matt 16:18). He does not need the help of a sympathetic secular government. However, he does need Christians committed to uncompromising holiness in their relationship with Him.

Jesus, who operated in total holiness with His Father, did not commit Himself to people's agendas, especially political ones (John 2:24, 25). Nevertheless, many of His followers, including His disciples, followed Him, thinking He was their savior from Roman rule, not the savior of their souls. When Pilot interrogated Christ, He responded by saying: "My kingdom is not of this world: if my kingdom were of this world, then would my servants fight, that I should not be delivered to the Jews: but now is my kingdom not from hence" (Joh 18:36).

A Christian's relationship with a civil government can get rather complicated, especially in a democracy that offers its citizens a voice in that government's operation. How involved should the Christians be in their government? I don't believe the Bible clearly defines that involvement other than to say that our primary commitment is to holiness with God. It also teaches that we must submit to civil authorities because God has ordained civil authority (Rom 13:1-7; I Pet 2: 13-15). However, when that civil government dictates that we, as citizens, violate moral law or requires us to compromise our holiness with God, it becomes our obligation to "obey God rather than man" (Act 5:29).

Another way Christians hinder the building of God's Kingdom is by not living in holiness or unity within the church body itself. In chapters four and five of Ephesians, Paul explains what he means by his desire to see the church "walk worthy" of its vocation. In discussing the marriage body, which we looked at in the previous chapter, Paul sums up his thoughts on the Church's worthiness in manifesting Christ's authority on earth. The essence of his argument in these two chapters is that to be worthy of our vocation, we must walk in complete unity and oneness, not only with God but also with each other. This two-fold quality of unity is what makes the Church holy.

I doubt whether many Christians would argue that we must walk in unity and oneness with God. However, few see the necessity of walking in unity and harmony with the people in the Church. An old saying aptly expresses this thought; "To live above with the saints we love, oh that will be glory, but to live below with the saints we know, now that's another story." Many verses in the Bible state that our relationship with God is intricately related to our relationship with people.

> "And the King shall answer and say unto them, Verily I say unto you, Inasmuch as ye have done *it* unto one of the least of these my brethren, ye have done *it* unto me." (Mat 25:40)

> "And when ye stand praying, forgive, if ye have ought against any: that your Father also which is in heaven may forgive you your trespasses." (Mar 11:25)

> "Therefore, if thou bring thy gift to the altar, and there rememberest that thy brother hath ought against thee; leave there thy gift before the altar, and go thy way; first be reconciled to thy brother, and then come and offer thy gift." (Mat 5:23-24)

"If a man says, I love God, and hateth his brother, he is
a liar: for he that loveth not his brother whom he hath
seen, how can he love God whom he hath not seen?"
(1Jn 4:20)

"Jesus said unto him, Thou shalt love the Lord thy God
with all thy heart, and with all thy soul, and with all thy
mind. This is the first and great commandment. And
the second *is* like unto it, Thou shalt love thy neighbor
as thyself." (Mat 22:37-39)

We cannot compartmentalize our relationship with God and our relationships with people into separate rooms of our lives and use different
rules for each. In the Spirit realm, there are no such compartments. It's
one big room, and the practice in one area of our lives affects every other
part. Our relationship with people affects our relationship with God, and
our relationship with God affects our relationship with people. If we do
not know that fact, we will live under the delusion that we can love one
and hate the other. It is not unusual for religious people to think that big-
otry, prejudice, and judging are okay. But concerning the religious zeal-
ots of his time, Christ said, "... except your righteousness shall exceed
the righteousness of the scribes and Pharisees; ye shall in no case enter into
the kingdom of heaven" (Mat 5:20). The Scribes and Pharisees built their
religion on rules. They had a rule for every area of life. Many of these
rules distorted the Levitical law and were very oppressive, especially to
the poor. If any rules were violated, severe punishment followed. It could
be said that both these groups were more into rules than relationships.
Jesus quickly rebuked them for how they treated their neighbors, the
poor, and women. Many of His parables, such as the Good Samaritan,
the Rich Man and Lazarus, the Parable of the Tenants, and others, aimed
to expose their hypocrisy. Christ's most descriptive characterization of
these groups was that they were "Whitewashed sepulchers." They were
clean on the outside but dead on the inside.

Many Christian churches today fit that exact description. From the
outside, they appear to be very pious. They have a form of Godliness but

deny its power. They all have their treasured lists of do's and don'ts and attend their churches with dutiful regularity. They are, however, quick to judge any person or Church outside of their denominational persuasion. I've heard them say things like, "You can't be a Catholic and be a Christian," or even, "You can't be a Democrat and be a Christian." Jesus tells us rules and religious viewpoints are not the defining characterizations of His body, the Church. In His last prayer before going to the cross, He prayed: "That they all may be one; as thou, Father, *art* in me, and I in thee, that they also may be one in us: that the world may believe that thou hast sent me. (Joh 17: 21, emphasis mine) Christ says in this verse that holiness within the Church authenticates that God sent Him and that He is not just another self-appointed world leader. However, it seems difficult for the Church to understand that this is true and that holiness is more important to God than religious rules.

As the body of Christ, many Christians claim that we cannot walk in unity unless we agree on every aspect of doctrine and practice. They use the concern of the prophet Amos to back up their claim. "Can two walk together, except they be agreed?" (Amos 3:3) But if you look at the meaning of the Hebrew word "yaad" (pronounced yaw-ad'), which is translated as "agreed," you will find that it means to meet or to engage. So, a more accurate translation of that verse would be, "Can two walk together, except they are agreed to walk together?" If we used the marriage body as an example, we would say, "Can two be married, except they agree to walk the road of marriage together?" If we claim that we must agree on every marriage issue, there would be no marriages. The same applies to the church body.

In his letter to the Corinthian Church, Paul made it quite clear that it was not total doctrinal agreement that he looked for in a church, but only whether they preached "Christ and Him crucified."

> "And I, brethren, when I came to you, came not with excellency of speech or of wisdom, declaring unto you the testimony of God. For I determined not to know anything among you, **save Jesus Christ, and him**

crucified. And I was with you in weakness, and in fear, and in much trembling. And my speech and my preaching *was* not with enticing words of man's wisdom, but in demonstration of the Spirit and of power: That your faith should not stand in the wisdom of men, but in the power of God." (1Co 2:1-5 emphasis mine)

Interestingly, Paul contrasts man's wisdom with God's power. That might seem to be a rather strange comparison. Isn't that like comparing apples and oranges? Not really. I believe that Paul understood God's wisdom to be powerful and man's wisdom to be weak.

We need to look at two men in the Old Testament who talked a great deal about wisdom to understand this comparison better. As you know, going through a period of horrific suffering, Job struggled to understand why this was happening. He tried discussing it with his friends and only got into debates about whether or not he was righteous. Finally, a young man named Elihu rebuked Job and his friends for trying to understand Job's predicament through human and religious wisdom. He said human understanding was inadequate and lacked the power to explain Job's life circumstances. After Elihu got done with Job, God started questioning him.

"Then the LORD answered Job out of the whirlwind and said, Who *is* this that darkeneth counsel by words without knowledge? Gird up now thy loins like a man; for I will demand of thee, and answer thou me. Where wast thou when I laid the foundations of the earth? Declare, if thou hast understanding" (Job 38:1-4).

When God finished His questioning, Job could only repent for thinking that his wisdom was adequate to answer all of the great questions of life. The other man, King Solomon, was humble enough, at first, to know he didn't have the human wisdom to run a kingdom, so he "wisely" asked God for wisdom. Because of that, he received God's wisdom and its power. He wrote: "The fear of God is the beginning of wisdom"

(Prov 9:10). However, after much success, he forgot that his power was a result of God's wisdom, not his own, and his power began a slow slide that ended up with his sons splitting the kingdom. Finally, he declared: "Therefore I hated life; because the work that is wrought under the sun *is* grievous unto me: for all *is* vanity and vexation of spirit" (Ecc 2:17).

It is easy to confuse our wisdom with God's wisdom and thereby lose God's power. So James gives us the best criteria to discriminate between human wisdom and God's wisdom when He says:

> "Who *is* a wise man and endued with knowledge among you? Let him shew out of a good conversation his works with meekness of wisdom. But if ye have bitter envying and strife in your hearts, glory not, and lie not against the truth. This wisdom descendeth not from above, but *is* earthly, sensual, and devilish. For where envying and strife *are,* there *is* confusion and every evil work. But the wisdom that is from above is first pure, then peaceable, gentle, *and* easy to be intreated, full of mercy and good fruits, without partiality, and without hypocrisy" (Jas 3:13-17).

All too often, it is the wisdom of man that robs the Church of its power. In the scripture above, James says that this kind of wisdom will only produce "bitter envying and strife," which will create "confusion and every evil work." To say that man's wisdom can run the Church says the Church can function smoothly without Christ. No, the head coordinates all of the body's activities. The body parts have no working connection except through the head. Therefore, the head produces holiness in the body, not the body itself.

The Church cannot experience the power of God except through the headship of Christ. Therefore, all communication within the body must, first of all, go through Christ. It is not our assignment to convince other church members that we are correct and that they are wrong. That is the work of the Holy Spirit. Our commitment, or agreement to walk together according to Amos 3:3, should be more durable than our need to agree on the "right doctrine." The quest for "right doctrine" has done nothing over the centuries except divide the Church and discredit it in the eyes of the world.

I realize that that last statement may offend many well-intentioned conservative Christians who place a high premium on orthodoxy. And I agree that we are all driven at times by the need to "be right." That is because we are all impregnated in both body and mind with the knowledge of good and evil. As a result, guilt has become the dominant force in our lives and mercilessly drives us to get it right. The Jewish leaders were so offended by Christ when he stated that He and the Father were "one" that they killed Him. Rightness, to them, trumped holiness. But to Christ, holiness was primary, if not everything. In His last prayer before his crucifixion, He did not ask the Father to make his followers righteous. No, He asked the Father to sanctify them to make them "one."

> "Sanctify them through thy truth: thy word is truth. As thou hast sent me into the world, even so, have I also sent them into the world. And for their sakes I sanctify myself, that they also might be sanctified through the truth. Neither pray I for these alone, but for them also which shall believe on me through their word; that they all may be one; as thou, Father, *art* in me, and I in thee, that they also may be one in us: that the world may believe that thou hast sent me. And the glory which thou gavest me I have given them; *that they may be one, even as we are one: I in them, and thou in me, that they may be made perfect in one*; and that the world may know that thou hast sent me, and hast loved them, as thou hast loved me." (John 17:17-23 emphasis mine)

Paul said that the Church's top priority must be holiness because holiness would ultimately protect the Church from manipulative false teachers.

> "Till we all come in the unity of the faith, and of the knowledge of the Son of God, unto a perfect man, unto the measure of the stature of the fulness of Christ: That we *henceforth* be no more children, tossed to and fro, and carried about with every wind of doctrine, by the sleight of men, *and* cunning craftiness, whereby they lie in wait to deceive; but speaking the truth in love, may grow up into him in all things, which is the head, *even* Christ:" (Eph 4:13-15)

Please do not get the idea from what I have said that righteousness is trivial to me. On the contrary, it is of utmost importance. However, the righteousness that originates in human wisdom is ever-changing, unstable, and very divisive. My concern is not that we disregard the matter of righteousness but that we put the horse before the cart and see holiness as God's way of producing that righteousness in us. Paul went even further when he declared that when we dwell in holiness with Christ, He allows us to participate in *His* wisdom, righteousness, sanctification, and redemption.

> "But of him are ye in Christ Jesus, who of God is made unto us wisdom, and righteousness, and sanctification, and redemption: That, according as it is written, He that glorieth, let him glory in the Lord." (1Co 1:30,31)

The apostle John also clarifies the relationship between holiness and righteousness by saying that *if* we walk in the light as Christ is in the light (or holiness), we are now in a relationship that allows His blood to cleanse us from all sin, making us righteous.

> "But if we walk in the light, as he is in the light, we have fellowship one with another, and the blood of Jesus Christ his Son cleanseth us from all sin. If we say that we have no sin, we deceive ourselves, and the truth is not in us. If we confess our sins, he is faithful and just

to forgive us *our* sins and to cleanse us from all unrighteousness." (1Jn 1:7-9)

Every human being desires to appear righteous before God and
others. So we try hard to hide, cover-up, suppress our flaws, and put on
a happy face, but inside, we are being destroyed by guilt. However, as we
commit to holiness with God, we will find the security in God's love and
forgiveness to face our sins and have them cleansed. Simply expressed,
righteousness is a fruit of holiness—not the cause of holiness.

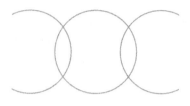

CHAPTER 8

THE HOLY ONE OF ISRAEL

When one thinks of God, capturing His essence with just one word or phrase is impossible. We say He is holy, righteous, loving, faithful, omnipotent, omniscient, omnipresent, eternal, gracious, a God of hope, and so on. The Old Testament Jews had at least fourteen names for God, each stressing different aspects of God's character. In this chapter, I will look at just one characteristic of God, expressed thirty times in the Old Testament – and twenty-five times by the prophet Isaiah alone. It is the phrase "the Holy One of Israel."

People often use the term "holy" to mean simply "super righteous." However, holiness and righteousness are two separate -- though inter-twined – characteristics of God. If God is righteous, He will also be holy; if He is holy, He will also be righteous.

Holiness, however, is a relational term and doesn't just refer to an individual's conduct. When holiness refers to God, it describes a God committed to existing in complete harmony within the holy trinity and with His creation. When it describes creation, holiness describes how people, objects, and times are set apart exclusively for God's use and purpose, as described in the following verses.

> "Ye have seen what I did unto the Egyptians, and *how* I bore you on eagles' wings and brought you unto myself. Now, therefore, if ye will obey my voice indeed, and

keep my covenant, then ye shall be a peculiar treasure unto me above all people: for all the earth *is* mine: and ye shall be unto me a kingdom of priests and a holy nation...." (Ex 19:4-6)

"And thou shalt take the anointing oil, and anoint the tabernacle, and all that *is* therein, and shalt hallow (sanctify) it, and all the vessels thereof: and it shall be holy." (Exo 40:9 emphasis mine)

"Remember the sabbath day, to keep it holy." (Exo 20:8)

In the seventeenth chapter of the Gospel of John, we read that Jesus sanctified himself so that He could, in turn, sanctify the church (verse 19). Sanctification is how something is set apart for holiness. Jesus was not saying He had to make Himself righteous so the church would be righteous. He was already wholly blameless. Instead, He set Himself apart to fulfill His Father's plan of atonement for sin. In willingly providing that atonement, Jesus removed the veil of spiritual blindness that separated man from God and allowed humanity to reenter a holy relationship with God.

"But their minds were blinded: for until this day remaineth the same vail untaken away in the reading of the Old Testament; which *vail* is done away in Christ." (2Co 3:14)

Righteousness, on the other hand, is a behavioral term. God is righteous in all that He does. Righteousness is behavior that aligns with the moral "rightness" of God. God does not want us to pursue righteousness through complying with rules but through a personal holy relationship. When we yield ourselves to God in holiness, we are privileged to participate in His divine nature (2 Pet 1:4), which includes His righteousness. Paul tells us that when we reconcile ourselves to God through holiness, He makes us righteous.

"Now then we are ambassadors for Christ, as though God did beseech *you* by us: we pray *you* in Christ's stead, be ye reconciled (sanctified) to God. He hath made him sin for us, who knew no sin; that we might be made the righteousness of God in him." (2Co 5:20,21)

Knowing what righteousness entails can separate us from God since a violation of moral rightness leaves us condemned by guilt. When we violate moral law, the resulting guilt will cause an encounter with a righteous God to be a terrifying experience. Adam and Eve hid and covered themselves because of the fear and guilt resulting from a violated moral conscience. The Israelites were terrified at Mt Sinai even to hear the voice of God. Jesus said people would not come to His spiritual light but preferred darkness because their deeds were evil (John 3:19, 20). So when we hide or suppress our unrighteousness because of guilt, we separate ourselves from God and can harm our bodies significantly. Dr. David R. Hawkins points out that suppressed guilt is the primary cause of all diseases and premature death in his writings.[9]

The knowledge of righteousness also becomes a weapon to attack and destroy others. When we wish to attack someone, we first look for some sin they have committed, which justifies our negative attitude toward them. Accusation and blame are the favorite weapons of all politicians. Working with people with criminal backgrounds, I have also learned that they will project their guilt onto those around them and become highly critical of other criminals. As a result, they alienate everybody around them and become very lonely and angry.

Then, there is the matter of self-righteousness when we attempt to convince people and God that we are better than we are. It rarely, if ever, works with people and never with God. Constantly comparing ourselves to others is a true expression of pride. The apostle Paul declared it to be highly unwise. Though we try to make ourselves feel more righteous than those around us through comparisons, the truth is that our unconscious

---

[9] Hawkins, David R, "Healing and Recovery"

guilt causes us to feel inferior to our peers. Therefore, we must do something to make ourselves look better or make our peers look worse.

Having distinguished holiness and righteousness, I will explore
why Isaiah portrayed God as "the Holy One of Israel" rather than the
"Righteous One of Israel." Both are true; however, I believe Isaiah chose
to emphasize God's holiness because holiness expresses a desire to restore and unite rather than judge and punish. He begins with a general
observation.

> "Ah sinful nation, a people laden with iniquity, a seed
> of evildoers, children that are corrupters: they have for-
> saken the LORD, they have provoked the Holy One
> of Israel unto anger, they are gone away backward."
> (Isa 1:4)

To understand this observation, we must go back in Israel's history
to the time of the exodus from Egypt. When Israel arrived at Mt Sinai,
God began to speak to them through Moses. He talked to them about
a new social order by which He would shape Israel into a nation unlike
any other nation. God desired that Israel would *not* be a class-conscious
society where certain people dominated and were numb to the needs
of the poor and hurting. In the Ten Commandments, He defined how
love for God and man should look. Then, with the Levitical law, God
spelled out the social responsibilities He expected of his people. He
instituted measures such as tithing, giving alms to the poor, and a
bond-servant program where the rich were to restore the "down and
outers" to respectability.

God did this to create a "holy" nation—a nation united with God
and each other, a nation in which all lives truly mattered, and a nation
in which no one focused solely on their own needs but also paid much
attention to the needs of others (Phi 2:4). God desired that Israel be set
apart (sanctified) to Him and set apart (sanctified) to each other. The
term "holy" became the watchword of the Levitical law, appearing 94
times. God's definitive command was, "For I *am* the LORD your God:

ye shall, therefore, sanctify yourselves, and ye shall be holy; for I *am* holy." (Lev 11:44)

Israel functioned quite well under this system of holiness in which God gave guidance through judges. But after a while, the people decided they wanted to be like the other nations and demanded a king despite God's warnings (I Sam 8:10-18). The holy relationship between Israel and God was adulterated with the installation of royalty and began to erode. Israel could no longer exist and split into two separate kingdoms. The kings now imposed their will on the people independently of God's leadership. They built their armies, conscripted young men and women to serve them, and confiscated animals and crops to support their lavish lifestyle. As a result, the classless society that flourished under holiness split into two classes of people: an elite political-religious class with all their appetites satiated and a lower class struggling to survive. Does that sound familiar?

By the time of Isaiah, all traces of holiness had disappeared. Instead, Isaiah observed a nation that had completely turned its back on God and abounded in every kind of sin and injustice. In his words, "they are gone away backward" from holiness with God and each other. Instead, they reverted to Egypt's social and political system, where the king set governmental and religious tones and enslaved the people.

Isaiah's call to Israel was not solely for social reform but for a return to holiness, leading to radical social reform. That is why he stressed a God of holiness rather than a God of righteousness. Isaiah echoed Leviticus's command: "Ye shall be holy; for I *am* holy." In the first 37 chapters, Isaiah lays out in much detail the results of a lack of holiness on Israel's part. These sinful conditions were the effect of the abandonment of holiness, not the cause. In the relationship between holiness and righteousness, holiness is always the cause, and righteousness is the result. The same is true of unholiness; it is the cause, and unrighteousness is the effect.

As we look at some of the verses that contain the phrase "The Holy One of Israel," we observe that Isaiah stresses Israel's rejection and abuse of the God who had delivered them from Egypt.

1. They forsook and provoked the Holy One of Israel. (1:4)
2. They blamed God for not moving fast enough to meet their needs. (5:19)
3. They cast away His laws and despised His word. (5:24)
4. They relied more on the nation defeating them than the Lord. (10:20)
5. They failed to see the greatness of God. (12:6)
6. They would not look to God for help. (17:7)
7. They found no joy in the Lord. (29:19)
8. They would not allow God to lead them. (30:11)
9. They had more trust in oppression and perverseness than in the word of God. (30:12)
10. They rejected that their real strength was the rest, quietness, and confidence they could have in God. (30;15)
11. They trusted Egypt's horses, chariots, and horsemen more than their God. (31:1)
12. They shouted and sneered at God. (37:23)

If any of us received the abuse God received, we would be provoked to anger and respond with righteous indignation. We would also feel justified in rejecting the offenders. That only shows that we place a higher value on righteousness than holiness. This is not the case with the "Holy One of Israel." Isaiah says that a holy God does not let grave offenses deter Him from His purpose and goal of restoring His children to holiness. In short, He has a passion for people. He shows this in the following verses, where He promises to restore Israel and exalt it in the eyes of the world.

1. "Fear not, thou worm Jacob, *and* ye men of Israel; I will help thee, saith the LORD, and thy redeemer, the Holy One of Israel." (41:14)
2. He promises to scatter their enemies. (41:16)
3. They will know that God did it, not they. (41:20)
4. He will give up other countries to save them. (43:3)
5. He will destroy Babylon to rescue them. (43:14)

6. He even invites them to ask Him what they want Him to do for them. (45:11)
7. He, the Lord of Host, is their redeemer (rescuer). (47:4)
8. He will lead them in a way that will cause them to profit. (48:17)
9. He will be like a husband who is rescuing his bride. (54:5)
10. He will glorify them in the eyes of other nations. (55:5)
11. He will return their sons and their wealth to them. (60:9)
12. Those who despise them will bow down to them. (60:14)

At first glance, it seems Old Testament writers portray a different God than New Testament writers. If you look strictly at God's activities in the Old Testament versus His actions in the New Testament, that would be easy to conclude. However, you will find an amazing consistency when you look at God from a holiness perspective and follow that theme throughout the Bible. The Holy One of Israel always has and will do whatever is necessary to rescue (redeem), restore, and glorify a people willing to walk in holiness with Him—often at the expense of those who rejected Him. In the Old Testament, God demonstrated a willingness to save and restore His people (Israel) and any aliens who wished to join with Israel in holiness, such as the Canaanite prostitute Hagar. He saved Noah with a flood. He rescued Lot with fire and brimstone; He recovered Abram after his father's death; He rescued Moses and Israel through the destruction of the Egyptian army; He saved Hagar at the expense of Jericho; and He rescued Israel multiple times at the cost of their conquerors. In the New Testament, God rescued the church at the expense of His Son. Ultimately, He will save His holy remnant (the church) at the cost of the world system. Because He is a holy God, He is a rescuing and redeeming God. Though His methods may change, His purpose will never change. I believe this is the God Isaiah proclaims to his fellow countrymen as the Holy One of Israel.

Today, we make a tremendous evangelical mistake by stressing that Christianity is primarily an escape from hell and entry into heaven. Instead, we should emphasize that it primarily involves engaging in a holy walk with God. Unfortunately, we seem to readily gloss over the many verses in the New Testament that call us to holiness with God and one another.

> "Sanctify them through thy truth: thy word is truth. And for their sakes, I sanctify myself, that they also might be sanctified through the truth. Neither pray I for these alone, but for them also which shall believe on me through their word; that they all may be one; as thou, Father, *art* in me, and I in thee, that they also may be one in us: that the world may believe that thou hast sent me. And the glory which thou gavest me I have given them; that they may be one, even as we are one:" (Joh 17:17-22)

> "I speak after the manner of men because of the infirmity of your flesh: for as ye have yielded your members servants to uncleanness and to iniquity unto iniquity; even so now yield your members servants to righteousness unto holiness." (Rom 6:19)

> "But now being made free from sin, and become servants to God, ye have your fruit unto holiness, and the end everlasting life." (Rom 6:22)

> "I, therefore, the prisoner of the Lord, beseech you that ye walk worthy of the vocation wherewith ye are called. With all lowliness and meekness, with longsuffering, forbearing one another in love; endeavoring to keep the unity of the Spirit in the bond of peace. *There is* one body and one Spirit, even as ye are called in one hope of your calling; one Lord, one faith, one baptism, one God and Father of all, who *is* above all, and through all, and in you all." (Eph 4:1-6)

"And that ye put on the new man, which after God is created in righteousness and true holiness." (Eph 4:24)

"For God hath not called us unto uncleanness, but unto holiness." (1Th 4:7)

"Follow peace with all *men,* and holiness, without which no man shall see the Lord:" (Heb 12:14)

"But as he which hath called you is holy, so be ye holy in all manner of conversation;" (1Pe 1:15)

"Because it is written, be ye holy; for I am holy." (1Pe 1:16)

The Holy One of Israel is still the Holy God of the Church, and though His methods may change because of the circumstances, His purpose will never change! He will constantly rescue those who wish to walk with Him in holiness from those who reject Him.

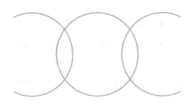

CHAPTER 9

WALKING IN THE SPIRIT

"There is therefore now no condemnation to them which are in Christ Jesus, who walk not after the flesh, but after the Spirit." (Rom 8:1)

"For what the law could not do, in that it was weak through the flesh, God sending his own Son in the likeness of sinful flesh, and for sin, condemned sin in the flesh: "That the righteousness of the law might be fulfilled in us, who walk not after the flesh, but after the Spirit." (Rom 8: 3,4)

"This, I say then, Walk in the Spirit, and ye shall not fulfill the lust of the flesh." (Gal 5:16)

"If we live in the Spirit, let us also walk in the Spirit." (Gal 5:25)

The reunion of God and His children through the atoning work of Christ has the potential to be the most powerful union on earth. In that union, God makes available to us all we need for life and godliness (2 Pet 1:3, 4), including the full power of God (Eph 6:10), the complete protection of God (Ps 4:8), and the complete guidance of God. (Jn16:13)

However, very few Christians have significantly experienced these aspects of God. We seem to flounder in life, struggling to find the peace and joy promised in the Bible. Much of the spiritual truth expressed in the Bible is nothing more than theological theory to most of us, with little or no reality. Indeed, "the gate is narrow, and the way is **hard** that leads to life, and those who find it are few." (Mat 7:14 ESV)

In the Bible, walking often expresses a process of claiming the promises of God and making them real in our lives. Claiming promises is not a one-time event. It is a process. It is a walk or a journey that requires faith, patience, and persistence to finish– one step at a time. To the Israelites, the land of Canaan represented the totality of God's promises to them. However, God did not automatically hand Canaan to them upon their arrival. Instead, they had to claim each parcel of ground step by step.

> "And the LORD thy God will put out those nations before thee by little and little: thou mayest not consume them at once, lest the beasts of the field increase upon thee." (Deu 7:22)

> "Every place whereon the soles of your feet shall tread shall be yours: from the wilderness and Lebanon, from the river, the river Euphrates, even unto the uttermost sea shall your coast be." (Deu 11:24)

The Canaanite nations resisted each step in that journey. In our journeys, these nations represent demonic forces that will try at every step to discredit the promises of God, hoping that we will get discouraged and quit walking. That is what Jesus meant when He said the road would be "hard." Unless we stand (Eph 6:14) on the promises of God and resist those demonic forces, those promises will never become a reality in our lives.

I must now go back to the first part of Jesus' statement, "the gate is narrow," and understand what He meant by that phrase. The generally accepted meaning of the gate is that it represents Christ or salvation. The narrow gate could also refer to holiness or oneness with Christ. Holiness is one of the Bible's most overlooked, misunderstood, and missed truths. We tend to walk past that gate because it's not lit with neon lights and flashing signs. It (the gate) is just the simple invitation to walk in unity with God, made possible through the atoning work of Christ and His Holy Spirit. When we accept that invitation to walk with God in holiness, we are opening a gate to a new life in which we are equipping ourselves to receive all God has for us. Many Christians try to appropriate those promises through religious rituals such as baptism or communion. These rituals can be helpful, but they often become an end in themselves rather than a means to an end. Leaders may not adequately explain the purpose of these rituals; therefore, people observe the practice only to comply with the church's traditions. All religious activity must lead you to that gate of holiness in Christ and is of little value to your spiritual growth if it doesn't.

True holiness- intimacy with God- is God's preferred way to instruct us in pursuing His promises. One of the Ten Commandments stated that God's people needed to set apart a time of Sabbath, one day out of the week, where they would cease all activity and just commune with God and listen for personal guidance. God reminded the Israelites of this commandment through the prophet Isaiah.

> "If thou turn away thy foot from (because of) the Sabbath, *from* doing thy pleasure on my holy day; and call the Sabbath a delight, the holy of the LORD, honorable; and shalt honor him, not doing thine own ways, nor finding thine own pleasure, nor speaking *thine own words*: Then shalt thou delight thyself in the LORD; and I will cause thee to ride upon the high places of the earth, and feed thee with the heritage of Jacob, thy father: for the mouth of the LORD hath spoken *it*." (Isa 58:13,14 insertion mine)

The story of the Israelites crossing the Jordan River into Canaan emphasizes the importance of holiness in claiming God's promises (Jos

4-5). They camped in Gilgal on the plain near Jericho, where God asked them to do three things: erect a monument of stones taken from the river Jordon, circumcise all of the males born in the desert, and celebrate their first Passover in Canaan. All of these activities had great spiritual significance. But they were insufficient to prepare them for taking possession of the land. One more thing was needed–holiness. In Jos 5:13-15, we find that Joshua met a stranger near Jericho.

> "And it came to pass, when Joshua was by Jericho, that he lifted up his eyes and looked, and, behold, there stood a man over against him with his sword drawn in his hand: and Joshua went unto him, and said unto him, *Art* thou for us, or for our adversaries?
>
> And he said, Nay; but *as* captain of the host of the LORD am I now come. And Joshua fell on his face to the earth, and did worship, and said unto him, What saith my lord unto his servant?
>
> And the captain of the LORD'S host said unto Joshua, Loose thy shoe from off thy foot; for the place whereon thou standest *is* holy. And Joshua did so." (Jos 5:13-15)

It would appear that Joshua understood what the man of God was saying because there was no discussion. He just complied with the order to remove his shoes as an act of submission with no comment. Maybe he had discussed the issue of holy ground with his mentor, Moses, over the past forty years and now understood what it meant. Moses was the only other man to have that experience. In both cases, God asked these men to do something they couldn't achieve without Him at their side. The Egyptians and Canaanites were not afraid of the Israelites, but they were terrified of the God of the Israelites. Without God, the Israelites would be powerless against the land's inhabitants.

The same is true about that problematic road we must walk today in claiming the promises of God. The devil and his demons are ever-present to block our way, causing us to doubt God's promises and directives. These demons are not afraid of us but terrified of our God. Therefore, our success in claiming the grace of God hinges on our awareness of God's holy presence in our lives, not on our religious rituals. Unless we agree to walk in the complete unity of holiness with God and all that it entails, we are doomed to discouragement and failure in our search for spiritual blessings. We cannot achieve success on our own.

In the gospel of Matthew, Jesus gives us a picture of what it means to walk in holiness with Him.

> "Come unto me, all *ye* that labour and are heavy laden and I will give you rest. Take my yoke upon you, and learn of me; for I am meek and lowly in heart: and ye shall find rest unto your souls. For my yoke *is* easy, and my burden is light." (Mat 11:28-30)

The Israelites were aware of how a yoke of oxen operated. Once two oxen were yoked together, they had no choice but to act as a team. The yoke, picturing holiness, became the controlling factor in their relationship. If they fought the authority of the yoke, they could severely injure themselves. However, if they summited to the yoke, they found great power and ability to accomplish things they could never do alone. For training purposes, a farmer would yoke a younger, undisciplined ox with an older ox that had learned submission to the yoke. Because of the yoke, the young ox finally learned to live and walk the life expected of him. Jesus was telling His followers that if they walked together with Him, yoked in holiness, he would guide their every footstep according to God's will and empower them to overcome all obstacles that would hinder their spiritual success. Yoked with Christ in holiness, we can echo the words of the apostle Paul when he said, "I can do all things through Christ which strengtheneth me." (Php 4: 13)

"Walking in the Spirit" means submitting to the yoke of holiness and letting the Spirit of God lead you in your spiritual walk. You notice that Jesus didn't tell those wanting to be spiritually powerful to join the local rabbinical school. No, He said, "Take my yoke upon you and learn of me." Today, many people who want to grow spiritually are urged to attend Christian Schools. I have no problem with that. However, doing so is no guarantee that they will live a holy life and find a life of spiritual power upon completion of schooling. I also find that many Christians who spend a lifetime sitting under the ministry of a highly academic pastor do not always come through that experience with a powerful spiritual life. They only have a lot of facts but no power. In the Apostle Paul's letter to his young protégé Timothy, he told him to avoid those Christian leaders who had only a form of godliness but denied its power. (2 Tim 3:5)

I was raised in a Christian home and attended churches that gave me tremendous knowledge of the Bible. As thankful as I am to have had such an upbringing, I never learned about the power of the Lord until I met a man named Johnny Johnson when I was twenty-two. Johnny was straightforward and humble but knew how to walk in the Spirit. I don't think I ever heard him preach expositorily from the Bible. His messages were simple faith stories about his daily experiences as he walked in holiness with God. The stories were breathtaking. I had never heard of such miracles except when reading the Bible. I remember wondering if it was possible that these miracles could be confirmed today. I could not deny that they were genuine in Johnnie's life; his stories stirred something in my soul. I began to pray for the kind of life I saw in Johnnie, and the Lord began to honor my prayers. It didn't happen overnight, but I started to see things happen in my life that I can only explain as miraculous. To tell you all of these stories would take several more chapters. Also, I've come to the point that I share these stories only with people who come to me looking for evidence of the power of God since people have accused me of boasting and bragging when I have shared these stories indiscriminately. My purpose in this book is not to spotlight the power of God in my own life but to help you find the key to seeing the power of God in *your* life. That key is holiness.

In the eighth chapter of Romans, Paul refers to "the law of the Spirit of life in Christ Jesus." Here, he is not talking about a law that we may find in a court of law but rather a law similar to the law of gravity in the natural world that explains how gravity works. Therefore, to better understand "walking in the Spirit," I will substitute the phrase "functioning in the Spirit" and explore this topic by using some examples of laws operating in the natural world.

We live in a material world governed by natural laws. Since the beginning, these laws have been operative and control how a natural phenomenon such as gravity operates. Merely living in a world of gravity does not mean we know how to function effectively. We must explore gravity and learn how it works— both its dangers and benefits. It is said that when a falling apple hit Isaac Newton, he wondered what made it fall. Out of that experience, he began investigating and discovering the "law of gravity," meaning he learned how gravity works. He found that gravity does not change; therefore, its nature can be expressed as law and described by a fixed mathematical formula. Because gravity doesn't change, we must conform to how it works. It will not conform to us. If you jump off a bridge, you will accelerate at 32 feet/sec/sec; after five seconds, you will fall at a velocity of 160 ft/sec. That translates to about 109 miles per hour. Gravity is a fixed law; you will die when you hit the water.

On the other hand, learning to utilize the law of gravity for good is very beneficial. For example, suppose you can harness the force with which gravity pulls water in a river downhill. In that case, you can use that force to turn electrical turbines and produce electrical energy for millions of people.

Another example is electricity. Humanity has always lived in a world of electricity. Electricity, like gravity, has always been a reality in nature. However, we have only recently been able to use it to enrich our lives through learning and conforming to how it works. Who would have dreamed only fifty years ago that we could talk to computers and get answers to almost any question we ask? But then, things like Siri and Alexis were only fantasies on Star Trek. Today, it is hard to imagine a world that could function without these realities. As with gravity, electricity can be both dangerous and beneficial. If you do not comply with the laws of electricity, it will kill you. However, If you understand the law that governs electricity and comply with it, there is no limit to the possibilities electricity will do for us.

When a person accepts God's invitation to be reconciled to Him (2 Cor 5:19-21), they have received an invitation to operate in the spirit world under the Holy Spirit's guidance. The spiritual world has always been a reality and will always be a reality, just like gravity and electricity in the natural world. The spiritual world operates according to "the law of the spirit of life in Christ," which will not change to accommodate us; we must conform to it. How does that work? The following verses give us an indication.

> "And said, If thou wilt diligently hearken to the voice of the LORD thy God, and wilt do that which is right in his sight, and wilt give ear to his commandments, and keep all his statutes, I will put none of these diseases upon thee, which I have brought upon the Egyptians: for I *am* the LORD that healeth thee." (Exo 15:26)

> "If ye be willing and obedient, ye shall eat the good of the land:" (Isa 1:19)

> "If ye abide in me, <u>and my words abide in you</u>, ye shall ask what ye will, and it shall be done unto you. Herein is my Father glorified, that ye bear much fruit; so shall ye be my disciples. As the Father hath loved me, so have I loved you: continue ye in my love. <u>If ye keep my commandments</u>, ye shall abide in my love; even as I have kept my Father's commandments, and abide in his love." (Joh 15:7-10 emphasis mine)

I believe we can function in the law of the Spirit of life in Christ, much like travelers utilize a GPS to guide them on a journey. They install the GPS in their car or as an app on their smartphone. It receives instructions from a satellite above and relays those instructions to us. <u>If we obey the GPS perfectly</u>, which is the key, traveling anywhere in the country can become very easy, and we will not get lost. Of course, we can still do it the old-fashioned way using maps, road signs, and people to guide us; however, there is a good chance of getting lost if we use these imperfect methods. I don't think I've ever navigated using old-fashioned techniques without getting lost at least once.

In the Old Testament, people got their spiritual guidance the old-fashioned way. They relied on the law as a road map and spiritual leaders such as Moses, Joshua, judges, and prophets to guide them in their spiritual walk. God did use these modalities and still uses the Bible and spiritual leaders today. However, when Jesus returned to heaven, He gave us a much superior form of guidance—the Holy Spirit. The Holy Spirit has always been with us and can still work through the written word and spiritual leaders; however, Jesus, at Pentecost, made the Holy Spirit available *in* each of us as our spiritual GPS to guide us through life. Whether we receive or use that guidance is up to us.

"And I will pray the Father, and he shall give you another Comforter, that he may abide with you forever; *Even* the Spirit of truth; whom the world cannot receive, because it seeth him not, neither knoweth him: but ye know him; for he dwelleth with you, and shall be in you." (Joh 14:16,17)

"But the anointing which ye have received of him abideth in you, and ye need not that any man teach you: but as the same anointing teacheth you of all things, and is truth, and is no lie, and even as it hath taught you, ye shall abide in him." (1Jn 2:27)

As Christ explained in John 10:10, the key to having a blessed and abundant life is total and complete obedience to the Holy Spirit's guidance on this earth. We don't have to wait for heaven to have a heavenly life. We can have a heavenly life on this earth. Christ prayed, "Thy kingdom come, Thy will be done on earth as it is in heaven."

Many Christians today seem to think that walking with God is only a matter of adopting a religious routine. We go to a particular place (a church or prayer closet) at a specific time and go through a prescribed religious ritual. I am not saying that we should ignore these activities, but based on everything I've just said, I would assert that these activities are not the end to which we should strive. When we see these activities as a means to adjust our walk to the law of the Spirit of life in Christ, they can certainly be helpful in our lives. However, only through a conformed and holy relationship with Christ, which He calls "the yoke," can we truly learn how to function productively in the spiritual world.

In the fourth chapter of John's gospel, John shares a story about Jesus that illustrates this point. In this story, Jesus encounters a Samaritan woman at Jacob's well. After a short conversation with Jesus, the woman perceives him as a prophet and asks him a question she has been pondering for some time. "Where should I worship, on the mountain in Samaria or Jerusalem?" Her question expresses that spirituality is related to a place of worship and that if you worshiped in a particular place, you might be more spiritual than in another place. So today, we might say: What church should I attend: Baptist, Catholic, Methodist, Pentecostal, Evangelical, or Unity? Christ's answer to her and us is that spirituality is not the function of a place of worship but on your walk with the Holy Spirit. Only the Holy Spirit can lead you into the reality of true worship.

> "Jesus saith unto her, Woman, believe me, the hour cometh, when ye shall neither in this mountain, nor yet at Jerusalem, worship the Father. Ye worship ye know not what: we know what we worship: for salvation is of the Jews. But the hour cometh and now is, when the true worshippers shall worship the Father in Spirit and in truth: for the Father seeketh such to worship him. God *is* a Spirit: and they that worship him must worship *him* in Spirit and in truth." (Joh 4:21-24)

The body of Christ today is deeply divided over doctrine and other religious rituals taught and practiced. Like the woman at the well, people sincerely seek the right church to worship, even though they often find the options overwhelming. Some churches have a good knowledge of the Bible and preach it wholeheartedly. Others may approach spiritually from more of a social or relational perspective. There are as many "flavors" of Christianity as churches; however, I believe they all have one thing in common. They all "know in part, and they prophesy in part" (1Co 13:9). As long as we are on this earth, no man, church, or denomination will have complete understanding and insight into spiritual truth. Therefore, it behooves us not to center our Christian fellowship solely on doctrinal agreement but on a mutual commitment to holiness with God and each other. Holiness is the door to blessing. Paul had only one criterion by which he decided whether he could fellowship with a church. It was whether they preached "Christ, and Him crucified." (I Cor 2:2). Jesus was telling this woman that God is not looking for worshipers based upon their theological correctness or completeness, but those who are genuinely demonstrating, in their daily walk, the reality of a life lived in holiness with God. Yes, knowing doctrine sometimes helps us in our quest for unity with God, as do some rituals. I do not wish to diminish doctrine's importance but only assert that doctrines must be seen as subservient to the higher purpose of holiness.

> "Give unto the LORD the glory due unto his name;
> worship the LORD in the beauty of holiness." (Psa 29:2)

Therefore, I must conclude that walking in the Spirit is the essence of holiness.

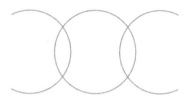

CHAPTER 10

THE BEAUTY OF HOLINESS

"Give unto the LORD the glory *due* unto his name: bring an offering, and come before him: worship the LORD in the beauty of holiness." (1Ch 16:29)

"And when he had consulted with the people, he appointed singers unto the LORD, and that should praise the beauty of holiness, as they went out before the army, and to say, Praise the LORD; for his mercy *endureth* forever." (2Ch 20:21)

"Give unto the LORD the glory due unto his name; worship the LORD in the beauty of holiness." (Psa 29:2)

Watching the news in the evening can be one of the most depressing events of my day. Between manipulative commercials and stories of the ugliest and most painful happenings on earth, it seems like the news media is trying to program my mind for depression and despair. However, they sometimes try to redeem themselves in the last two minutes by sharing a feel-good story. This story is of someone- usually a child- who did something sacrificial or beneficial for people around them. It feels like a spark of decency and beauty in a world of darkness and reminds us there are still people who are aware of their connection to something larger than themselves –humanity. It is that awareness of connectedness to humanity that, in a small way, exemplifies the beauty of holiness as God envisioned it on this earth.

If we don't understand holiness, it is impossible to describe its beauty. Therefore, I must clarify again what I believe holiness to be. I have said that holiness is not a behavioral term such as righteousness but a relational expression. It describes a God committed to existing in complete unity and harmony within the holy trinity and His creation. When referring to humanity, it describes people committed to complete identity with and obedience to God and unity with God's children. When Peter quotes the Levitical law as saying, "Be ye holy, for I am holy" (1Pe 1:16), he could have said it this way; be ye set apart from the world and conformed to God and His will, for He is wholly committed to you. Jesus expressed holiness this way; "Believe me that I *am* in the Father, and the Father in me: or else believe me for the very works' sake" (Joh 14:11)

We live in a physical world, making it difficult to understand that kind of spiritual oneness or holiness. The laws of physical science tell us that two pieces of matter cannot occupy the same space simultaneously. Also, all substances have sizes and shapes. However, we can still demonstrate holiness as we see God's various expressions of beauty in the physical world. We can observe that all the components of nature come together to form something beautiful. Whether it is a flower, a sunrise or sunset, a lake, the fall colors, cloud formations, deserts, or jungles, they all reflect a sense of naked beauty that inspires us. Paul says that nature expresses God in the same way art reflects the artist. (Rom 1:20) God's unity expressed in nature reflects the beauty of God's holiness and is always inspiring. Although people can create beauty, man's creations are never bigger and grander than God's.

In the spiritual world, however, the expression of holiness is somewhat different than in the physical world. All spiritual reality transcends time and space. One cannot limit spirituality to a place such as a church, prayer closet, or time. It is experienced at all times and in all areas. Therefore, we cannot divide our spiritual lives into separate worlds and say we are more spiritual in church and less spiritual out-side. We are who we are all the time and in all places. People who compartmentalize their spiritual lives by acting one way in church and another at work are perceived as hypocritical. In the above verse, Jesus is saying that true holiness (I in the Father and the Father in me) can only be authenticated by the righteous behavior that it produces (the works), not by the impressions we try to make on people through our religious lives.

We see the opposite of holiness today: separation and division in every sector of our lives. While holiness is the dominant characteristic of the Spirit, separation is the chief characteristic of our fleshly nature or ego. The apostle Paul states:

> "And I, brethren, could not speak unto you as unto spir-itual, but as unto carnal, *even* as unto babes in Christ. I have fed you with milk, and not with meat: for hitherto ye were not able *to bear it,* neither yet now are ye able. For ye are yet carnal: for whereas *there is* among you envying, and strife, and divisions, are ye not carnal, and walk as men? For while one saith, I am of Paul; and another, I *am* of Apollos; are ye not carnal?" (1Co 3:1-4)

According to the ego, we cannot view ourselves as being in a holy union with someone else because that would require that our ego yield to another ego's desires. Unless our ego perceives itself as gaining something through submission to other egos, it will never yield. Giving and compli-ance equate to losing while taking, fighting, and dominating represent a gain to the ego. Unless the ego perceives itself as getting the better end of the deal, the deal won't happen. Paul says that this egotistical way of thinking is how the wisdom of this world operates.

> "Let no man deceive himself. If any man among you seemeth to be wise in this world, let him become a fool, that he may be wise. For the wisdom of this world is foolishness with God. For it is written, He taketh

the wise in their own craftiness. And again, The Lord
knoweth the thoughts of the wise, that they are vain.
Therefore let no man glory in men...." (1Co 3:18-21)

James concurs with Paul and explains that implementing worldly
wisdom will produce gruesome results.

"But if ye have bitter envying and strife in your hearts,
glory not, and lie not against the truth. This wisdom
descendeth not from above, but *is* earthly, sensual, and
devilish. for where envying and strife *is,* there *is* confusion and every evil work." (Jas 3:14-16)

One must ask, "Why can't rational people see this?" Why can't we
see that all human problems originate from a mindset of apposition and
competition rather than unity? It is me against you and you against me.
We fight for survival rather than cooperate for survival. According to
the ego, I can only win by taking something from you and vice versa.
Our human lives are built on the foundation of competitiveness, from
athletic entertainment to the atrocities of war. We are seemingly blind
to another way of living and relating that thrives on unity and holiness.
Paul says the God of this age has blinded our eyes to the truth (2 Cor
4:4, 1 Jon 2:11), and because of the blindness of our hearts, we are alien-
ated from the life of God available to us. (Eph 4: 18) We live in a dream
world, thinking it is a reality. Unfortunately, it is not reality; we must
be awakened to experience reality.

"Wherefore he saith, Awake thou that sleepest, and
arise from the dead, and Christ shall give thee light."
(Eph 5:14)

As we look at the world today (2022), in which we see an abundance
of egotistical "worldly wisdom," only one word can accurately summarize most of what is happening in the world—ugly. It is a nightmare.

So, what would a life based on unity and holiness look like if we awoke to it? The following examples will give us some insight into such a life.

*   *   *

> *"Is* not this the fast that I have chosen? To loose the bands of wickedness, to undo the heavy burdens, and to let the oppressed go free, and that ye break every yoke? *Is it* not to deal thy bread to the hungry, and that thou bring the poor that are cast out to thy house? When thou seest the naked, that thou cover him; and that thou hide not thyself from thine own flesh? (Isa 58:6,7)

In these verses, God is saying through Isaiah that He desires us to identify with and help those victims whom society has relegated to second or third-class citizens for one reason or another. God is saying here that the "fast" should not be used as a pity party to get God's attention but as an opportunity to share the blessings of God with those who have never seen them. When we see oppression, we speak for the oppressed. When we see hunger, we share our food. When we see homelessness, we share our homes. When we see nakedness, we give them the shirt off our backs. The world may call that socialism, but God calls it love. Phillip Yancey calls this "seeing upside down."

> "Taking God's assignment seriously means that I must learn to look at the world upside down, as Jesus did. Instead of seeking out people who stroke my ego, I find those whose egos need stroking; instead of important people with resources who can do me favors, I find people with few resources; instead of the strong, I look for the weak; instead of the healthy, the sick. Is not this how God reconciles the world to himself? Did Jesus not

insist that he came for the sinners and not the righteous, for the sick and not the healthy?"[10]

*   *   *

"Behold, how good and how pleasant *it is* for brethren to dwell together in unity! *It is* like the precious ointment upon the head, that ran down upon the beard, *even* Aaron's beard: that went down to the skirts of his garments; as the dew of Hermon, *and as the dew* that descended upon the mountains of Zion: for there, the LORD commanded the blessing, *even* life for evermore" (Psa 133:1-3).

Unity does not mean we have to agree on everything to have God's blessing, but rather that we are committed to walking together as in marriage. Such a commitment requires that we learn to love, forgive, listen, be humble, put up with, have self-control, have faith in each other, and be gentle. The world will view us as weak, but God says that we will see His anointing and blessing in our lives when we do this.

*   *   *

"But love ye your enemies, and do good, and lend, hoping for nothing again; and your reward shall be great, and ye shall be the children of the Highest: for he is kind unto the unthankful and *to* the evil. Be ye therefore merciful, as your Father also is merciful. Judge not, and ye shall not be judged: condemn not, and ye shall not be condemned: forgive, and ye shall be forgiven: Give, and it shall be given unto you; good measure, pressed down, and shaken together, and running over, shall men give into your bosom. For with the same measure

---

[10] Yancey, Philip. Grace Notes (p. 25). Zondervan. Kindle Edition.

that ye mete withal it shall be measured to you again"
(Luk 6:35-28).

The world says that when you come against evil, you must fight and destroy the evil before it destroys you. Many Christians have bought into this mentality because it is how the fleshly or egotistical mind thinks. However, Christ is stating what we call the "rule of reciprocity," which says that treating people in a certain way strongly influences how they reciprocate to you. For example, if you extend a hand in fellowship, you affect them to extend their hand in response. The rule of reciprocity works with good behavior as well as bad. I almost learned this the hard way when I was a new teacher many years ago. The students asked me to chaperone the first high school dance of the year. I was strong and athletic in my younger years and thought I could whip anybody on the planet. That evening, a group of young ruffians who were not students tried to crash the dance. Being young and self-inflated, I wanted to intimidate them into leaving. However, they were not intimidated and were about to challenge me when a much older and wiser parent stepped in. He calmly talked them down briefly and convinced them to leave. I was amazed at how his calm and non-threatening demeanor worked when my tough-guy act had failed. I was also very thankful when I learned the guy challenging me was a Golden Gloves champion of Lansing, Michigan.

*   *   *

"And he answering said, Thou shalt love the Lord thy God with all thy heart, and with all thy soul, and with all thy strength, and with all thy mind; and thy neighbour as thyself. And he (Jesus) said unto him, Thou hast answered right: this do, and thou shalt live."(Luk 10:27,28)

Would not this world be a beautiful place in which to live if we loved others as much as we love ourselves? For Christians, this is not a suggestion but a command. The Apostle John says that if we cannot treat other

humans in love, we fool ourselves by thinking we love God. Loving God
and hating people is just another example of spiritual compartmental-
ization. It is hypocritical and false Christianity. Paul goes further when
he says we should view others as being *better* than ourselves. (Php 2:3)
When I see people on social media use the foulest possible language to
demean and belittle people they disagree with, it is hard to imagine that
they would even want to go to heaven when they die. Heaven is a place
of beautiful love and harmony.

*   *   *

The twelfth chapter of Romans is what I like to call "the litany of
a transformed life." I have chosen not to print the whole chapter; however, you might do well to read it independently. The various behaviors
Paul lists in this chapter picture a spiritually beautiful person who has
appropriated God's grace and personifies a life of holiness. Verses three
through eight, especially verse five, speak directly to holiness and how
we serve the body of Christ with our unique gifts. The rest of the chapter
describes how the transformed Christian operates counter to the specta-
cle in much of the world's culture.

*   *   *

"I, therefore, the prisoner of the Lord, beseech you that
ye walk worthy of the vocation wherewith ye are called,
with all lowliness and meekness, with longsuffering,
forbearing one another in love; endeavoring to keep the
unity of the Spirit in the bond of peace. *There is* one
body and one Spirit, even as ye are called in one hope
of your calling; One Lord, one faith, one baptism, One
God and Father of all, who *is* above all, and through all,
and in you all." (Eph 4:1-6)

In this scripture, Paul points out that holiness genuinely sets the
church apart from the world and makes it worthy to speak on God's

behalf. Therefore, as separation and competitiveness define relationships in the world, holiness must define the church.

* * *

"Fulfil ye my joy, that ye be likeminded, having the same love, *being* of one accord, of one mind. *Let* nothing *be done* through strife or vainglory, but in lowliness of mind, let each esteem others better than themselves. Look not every man on his own things, but every man also on the things of others" (Php 2:2-4).

We all know that Paul saw preaching the gospel as his ministry's primary goal, letting nothing distract him from that mission. However, he did not consider evangelism the end of his duty. Once he birthed a new life in Christ, he saw himself as a spiritual parent whose responsibility was to see his children grow up into the image of Christ. There is great joy in seeing a newborn child, but the great fulfillment of a parent's joy is to see that child grow into a mature and successful adult. The success of a child is always the crowning joy of a parent. According to this scripture, Paul's crowning joy was to see his spiritual children walk in holiness—being of one accord and one mind.

Do not these scriptures describe a gracious, beautiful world in which to live? However, such a world would seem more romantic than realistic to most. They might even say such a world would be pure fantasy. That is because the fleshly mind (ego) cannot envision a life of holiness. Therefore, the righteousness described in these verses can only proceed from minds transformed by the grace of God through holiness that see themselves as one with God and our brothers and sisters.

I want to close this chapter by looking at a story from the twentieth chapter of the book of Second Chronicles about King Jehoshaphat, the King of Judah. He received the news that a vast army of soldiers from three different regions in Edom was approaching Judah from the Southeast to start a war. The writer of the Chronicles does not give the reason for the invasion; however, he does mention that Syria, their constant nemesis, may have had something to do with it. There was also the fact that Israel (the ten tribes) had allowed the armies passage as far North as the town of Engedi on the West bank of the Dead Sea, indicating their support for the invasion.

What happens next should be a pattern of how we respond in fearful situations with the beauty of holiness. So it says, "And Jehoshaphat feared, and set himself to seek the LORD, and proclaimed a fast throughout all Judah" (2Ch 20:3). How many times do we fear and seek **our** solutions, neglecting the presence and wisdom of a Holy God and end up paying a painful price? Yet, seeking God is the greatest blessing of holiness. He is here. As Christ said, He is in me, and I am in Him. In holiness, our battles are His battles (vs. 15), our problems are His problems, and His solution can be our solution if we truly trust Him.

As a result of Jehoshaphat's decision to seek God, Judah came together and sought God as a nation. "And all Judah stood before the LORD, with their little ones, their wives, and their children" (2Ch 20:13). This was one of the few times that the Jewish people honored God's directive to be a holy nation– to be one with Him and one with each other. As a result, He was faithful in answering their prayers with His solution, as unconventional as it must have seemed to them. God told them through the prophet that they would find the invaders (vs.16) but wouldn't have to fight (vs.17) because the battle is not theirs, but God's (vs.15). If the first step in overcoming fear is to seek God, the second step is to wait for God's answer. Don't move until you hear from God. Actions motivated by fear are seldom, if ever, rational actions. However, actions resulting from waiting for God's answer will reflect God's wisdom.

Once you have received God's solution to the problem, you are ready for step three. I warn you, however, that the only test of whether you have received "God's answer" is that you will have a strange sense of peace. So, until that peace arrives in your heart, keep praying. "And let the peace of God rule in your hearts…" (Col 3:15). When that peace comes, you are ready for step three: stop praying and start praising. The answer has become a reality in your heart by faith, even though it has not yet outwardly manifested.

> "And Jehoshaphat bowed his head with *his* face to the ground: and all Judah and the inhabitants of Jerusalem fell before the LORD, worshipping the LORD.
>
> And the Levites, of the children of the Kohathites, and of the children of the Korhites, stood up to praise the LORD God of Israel with a loud voice on high." (2Ch 20:18,19)

The last step in this pattern involves validating your faith through obedience. As in Eph 6, we must stand if God tells us to stand. As in Ps 46:10, we must be still if He tells us to be still. If He tells us to observe the enemy and then be still, as in this story (vs.16), we must observe and be still.

The following day, Jehoshaphat discussed among the people how to carry out the Lord's command (vs. 21). It is interesting to me that Jehoshaphat didn't decide himself how to carry out the Lord's command. Walking in holiness, he submitted to the people and listened to them. Involving the people in a decision is a step that many pastors fail to take. Instead, they gather a board that will agree with them and then dictate to the church their desired action. I don't think this is an expression of holiness in the church. Watchman Nee, the great Chinese theologian, states in one of his books that if the church does not amen the pastor, the pastor should repent. Holiness involves the whole church body. In Jehoshaphat's case, it was not just Jehoshaphat responding to God but the entire nation. What a beautiful picture of holiness. As a result, after consulting with the people, Jehoshaphat "appointed singers unto the LORD, and that should praise the beauty of holiness, as they went out before the army, and to say, Praise the LORD; for his mercy *endureth* forever."

I would love to end this chapter on that high note; however, the story doesn't end here. In verse 22, the writer exclaims that when the singers start singing, God sets ambushes "against the children of Ammon, Moab, and mount Seir, which were come against Judah; and they were smitten." So, he caused them to ambush each other. In this story, we see the juxtaposition between the results of Judah's holiness and their enemies' separateness. As Judah submitted themselves in holiness to God and each other, they were victorious without fighting. However, when God released the children of Ammon, Moab, and Mount Seir to their fundamental selfish nature, they destroyed each other.

As I read this story, I cannot help but reflect on two institutions of our American culture that are both dear to me—our government and the Christian church. Our founding fathers dreamed of establishing America as "one nation under God." That sounds like holiness. However, holiness requires that all parties in the union recognize God as the only authority that can hold it together. That, by definition, is not a democracy. It is a Theocracy. Without mutual submission to each other and to God, there can be no true holiness, only tentative agreements based on common goals. Unfortunately, the shared goals and dreams of America's founding fathers (equality, justice for all, life, liberty, and pursuit of happiness), some of the fruits of holiness, have never proved to be a reality for the masses in America. The main reason is that our founders never envisioned the increasing number of ethnic minorities contributing to our country's diversity and the ethnic prejudices that would ensue, making it virtually impossible to have unity. Also, considering what is best for the nation (statesmanship) has given way to what is best for me (politics). Governmental leadership has become a viciously aggressive war between parties and various social movements that develop in society. If this style of government continues to function as it has in the last few decades, one could wonder whether our democracy can survive.

The best possibility for holiness to function in America must begin in the church. Paul says that holiness in the church makes it worthy to carry on its purpose of exposing God's "Zoe" life to the world. (Eph 4:1-18) Sadly, the church in America does not realize its natural beauty is not found in its cathedrals, megachurches, sacraments, political clout, or narrow doctrines and rules. It is to be found in its ability to love God and people.

> "And, behold, a certain lawyer stood up, and tempted him, saying, Master, what shall I do to inherit eternal life? He said unto him, What is written in the law? How readest thou? And he answering said, Thou shalt love the Lord thy God with all thy heart, and with all thy soul, and with all thy strength, and with all thy mind; and thy neighbour as thyself. And he said unto him, Thou hast answered right: this do, and thou shalt live. (Luk 10:25-28)

This summation of the Levitical law and its manifestation through Christ's life and death is the essence of what is beautiful about holiness. Therefore, Paul said that the only message of the Christian church should be "Christ and Him crucified" (I Cor 2:2). As Christ became a counter-cultural influence to the religious-political forces of His day, so should the church (His body) let the beauty of its holiness serve as salt and light to the culture in which we live.

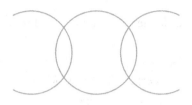

CHAPTER 11

THE POWER OF HOLINESS

"This know also, that in the last days perilous times shall come. For men shall be lovers of their own selves, covetous, boasters, proud, blasphemers, disobedient to parents, unthankful, **unholy**, without natural affection, trucebreakers, false accusers, incontinent (no self-control), fierce, despisers of those that are good, traitors, heady, high-minded, lovers of pleasures more than lovers of God; having a form of godliness, but **denying the power** thereof: from such turn away (2Ti 3:1-5 emphasis mine)

In the verses above, Paul describes the many fleshly or egotistical attitudes that will dominate people's minds in the end times. You will notice that Paul lists unholiness among them. He implies that these attitudes will form the foundation for a very turbulent and dangerous state of affairs. People will use forceful arguments, threats, and abuse to achieve their purposes instead of love, compassion, and empathy. Separation and competition between people will cause them to attack each other rather than cooperate. Using force will produce a counterforce, canceling or limiting any good they may have intended. As a result, little to nothing is accomplished.

A relatively benign example of this competition occurred when I was in college. We held an event in the fall called the Freshman Sophomore Pull. It was a tug-of-war between two teams across the Black River in Holland, Michigan. These two teams trained harder than the school football team. When the big day came, each team dug foxholes on their side of the river to keep them from sliding and giving them greater leverage. Each team's captain would bark out signals to keep them operating together for maximum force. These pulls could last for hours before one team wore the other down and pulled them into the river. When I looked at our team members, I saw exhausted bodies and extreme physical pain. Ultimately, the result was always the same—one team got wet. My freshman team won the first and only pull I attended, and we had bragging rights for the rest of the year. We trumpeted that we had dumped the other team in the river. It is easy to boast about defeating someone else because that's how the ego works. The ego never functions to enhance and enrich others' lives, only to pull them down.

Defeating someone may seem like good, clean fun in an athletic competition. But if we see this type of competition in governments, churches, or marriages, it is no longer fun but often dreadfully destructive. In our legislatures, Democrats and Republicans find it almost impossible to cooperate on anything that might enhance the American people's lives. Instead, they feel they must forcefully oppose and degrade the other party, no matter the issue, thereby canceling or minimizing most legislation before them. As a result, they expend tremendous energy with minimal effects. In essence, our legislators have denied the intrinsic power of democracy, which shows respect for people who see things differently and use those differences to arrive at a more complete view of the issue. Instead, they have resorted to the hostile force and counterforce of political warfare to discredit all opinions but theirs. They have devolved from statesmanship to using political force. In the scripture above, Paul says that in the end times, people will prefer egotistical competition and the use of force to achieve their goals rather than the power of godliness and holiness. We have devolved from holiness and unity to a "survival of the fittest" mentality.

I don't think any Christian would openly say that godliness is powerless. However, when it comes to reality, our ego asserts that we can achieve more through force than we can by resting in the power of God and operating in love. Opposing others through force is the foremost strategy of the ego. By choosing conflict over cooperation, it ignores the power of holiness.

At this point, I need to distinguish what I mean by force and what I call power. These terms can mean many different things to different people. For my purpose, I will limit the discussion of these topics to human relationships. In this context, force is a human act or attitude that prefers to influence others in a dominant or coercive manner. On the other hand, power denotes an inner strength that attracts people by its desire to create and enhance life through unity, love, compassion, and grace. Jesus epitomized the distinction between power and force when He declared, "The thief cometh not, but to steal, kill, and destroy (force): I have come that they might have life and that they might have *it* more abundantly" (power) (Joh 10:10, emphasis mine). Paul also draws a similar contrast of force and power when He states, "God hath not given us the spirit of fear (a demonic type of force), but of power, and of love, and of a sound mind" (2Ti 1:7). It would appear that the devil, working through the fleshly nature of people, is always trying to supplant the power of holiness in our lives with an array of fleshly forces such as fear, anger, guilt, and apathy, to name a few. Paul explains this phenomenon in the seventh chapter of Romans. He explains that when he intended to do something good, an opposing force in his body was attempting to neutralize his positive, loving intent. His final cry is one of despair– "Oh wretched man that I am! Who shall deliver me from this body of death" (Rom 7:24)? He repeats that thought to the Galatian church when he states:

> "For the flesh lusteth against the Spirit, and the Spirit
> against the flesh: and these are contrary the one to the
> other: so that ye cannot do the things that ye would."
> (Gal 5:17)

We deny the power of holiness because we lack faith that it is adequate to overcome the evil in this world. Is "turning the other cheek" more potent than retaliating (Matt 5: 39)? Can we overcome evil with good (Rom 12: 21)? When we refuse to believe that prayer is more potent than partisan politics, we will seek politicians to solve our problems rather than falling to our knees and repenting (2 Ch 7: 14). Many Christians do not practice prayer enough to understand how it works as a progenitor to holiness. As a result, prayer is woefully missing as a corporate activity in the Christian Church. Where churches have regularly scheduled prayer meetings, they are the worst attended meetings in the church.

The power of God manifested through holiness is illustrated in the Old Testament book of Joshua. As the story goes, God rescued Israel from slavery in Egypt to build a nation in Canaan based on holiness. God worked miracle after miracle in delivering Israel from the Egyptian army and physically sustaining them in the desert. However, when they spied out the land of Canaan, they were overcome with fear by the size of the people there and refused to trust the power of God to overcome them. Later, the Canaanites beat them badly when they attempted to invade the land independently against God's command, and God sent them back into the desert. Forty years later, God brought them to the Jordan River's east side to give them a second chance to fulfill their destiny.

This time, God guided them through some basic steps critical to success. First, God admonished Joshua three times to "be of good courage" as he prepared to enter Canaan the second time. This command implied the journey ahead would not be a stroll in the park. It would be fraught with many obstacles and much resistance, requiring courage. Christ reminds us today that our spiritual journey will resemble Joshua's. It will come at a cost to us– not the price He paid on the cross to give us access to that road, but the price we must pay to finish the journey. That cost involves the courage to let go of our confidence in our flesh and trust in the power of God. I call it "Letting go and letting God."

"And whosoever doth not bear his cross, and come after me, cannot be my disciple. For which of you intending to build a tower, sitteth not down first, and *counteth the cost*, whether he have sufficient (courage) to finish it? Lest haply, after he hath laid the foundation, and is not able to finish it, all that behold it begin to mock him, saying, This man began to build and was unable to finish." (Luk14:27-30 emphasis mine)

Courage requires an objective view of our present condition and a willingness to accept future possibilities. For example, in AA, one must have the courage to admit to being an alcoholic and be committed to the opportunities for change before he can progress through the program. Likewise, in marriage counseling, each spouse must have the courage to face the truth about their contribution to their marital dysfunction and be committed to change before they can be helped. John states that confession, or acknowledgment of sin, must precede the forgiveness and cleansing of sin. (I Jn 1: 9)

The first step to any spiritual journey must be the courage to face the truth about oneself. Jesus states, "And this is the condemnation, that light (truth) is come into the world, and men loved darkness rather than light (truth) because their deeds were evil." (Joh_3:19 emphasis mine) Then He said, "I am the way, the truth, and the life: no man cometh unto the Father, but by me." (Joh 14:6) In these verses, Jesus equates Himself to "truth and light" so that coming to Christ equates to coming to the truth, or light. He is spiritual truth and light. We must have faith in Christ's ability and desire to deal with our spiritual condition in much the same way that we must trust doctors before we allow them to deal with our physical problems. Christ is not looking for a reason to destroy us but a way to help us on our journey. We can trust Him.

Once God impressed Joshua with the need for courage, He had to instill courage in the people. To do this, He commanded Joshua to lead Israel across the Jordan River while it was flooding – symbolizing baptism. In baptism, God buried their past and asked the people to let go of the mindsets they acquired in the desert and Egypt before preparing them for a new life. (Jos 5:9). I will say that baptism does take great courage when we understand what God is trying to accomplish through it. God is asking us to have enough courage to let go of our past and open ourselves up to possibilities before us. It can be a turning point in our lives.

Once the Israelites passed through the river and before its waters returned to their usual flow, God commanded Joshua to take twelve rocks from where Israel had come and construct a monument on the river floor. This monument represented their past life to be buried in the river. Then, He commanded them to take twelve stones from the river bottom and build a memorial on the west side of the river to represent their new life and to show future generations what God had done for them. God then released the waters once they completed that task, thus burying their past.

Next, God ordered them to circumcise the new generation born in the desert (signifying that they were still God's covenant people) and to celebrate their first Passover in their new home (signifying that they were still forgiven people). Upon completing these rituals, the people needed one more step to empower them to move forward and claim the land. That step was not a better understanding of the land as one might think. Joshua already knew the land since he was one of the twelve spies sent out by Moses forty years before. This time, God would expose Joshua and the people to the power of holiness. (Jos 5:13-15)

While standing on Jericho's plains, Joshua met the "captain of the host of the Lord," who informed him that he was standing on holy ground. God wanted him to know that he was not alone in this endeavor. God was standing with him in holiness. You are standing on holy ground when you believe God is one with you both in will and action, never leaving or forsaking you. In holiness, our resolve is not empowered by our desires alone but also by God's desires. This holy resolve caused Paul to tell the Philippian church that he could "do all things through Christ who strengthened him" (Php 4:13).

Holiness is the most potent power on earth regarding our relationship with God. It brings together the availability of human beings and God's limitless power. Two illustrations in the Old Testament demonstrate what can happen when we *do not* walk in holiness with God and when we *do*. In the first case, Asa, king of Judah, was tormented by King Baasha of Israel. Instead of looking to God to help him, Asa went to Benhadad, the king of Syria, and made a pact with him, paying Benhadad a great deal of money to take care of his problem. God was furious over Asa's choice and sent Hanani, a seer, to give Asa a message. That message was that God was looking for a person through whom He could show Himself strong. Since Asa rejected that strength, God said that from now on, Benadad would be Asa's problem, and Asa's future would be a constant war (2 Chr 16:9).

In the second illustration, we see Jehoshaphat, who, when faced with a confederation of enemies, called a nation prayer meeting and sought God's answer. Upon getting God's answer, Jehoshaphat put the choir out in front of the army to praise God for the beauty of holiness. The result was that God caused the enemy to destroy themselves (2 Chr 21-23).

On the one hand, a person who denies or neutralizes God's power does so because of their lack of faith in God's ability, as demonstrated by Asa. Instead, they choose to rely on their strategies and skills to resolve problems. They get angry and find ways to attack other people, hoping they can overpower their opponents and succeed through their resources. On the other hand, those who walk in holiness with God relinquish their forcefulness in favor of God's power. Yes, each scenario requires action, but in the first case (Asa), the action resulted from man's wisdom. In the second case (Jehoshaphat), the action resulted from obedience to God.

King Asa was a man who walked after the dictates of his heart. He illustrates that holiness cannot function in a person who walks in the flesh or the ego realm. Holiness can only operate in the realm of the spirit. A holy God will not cooperate with a fleshly or egotistical person like Asa. He resists the proud and gives grace to the humble. Also, two fleshly people can not walk in true holiness because the ego doesn't believe in holiness. It believes in separateness. The ego forms self-serving relationships that seek gain at the expense of others. The association will fail if the other person does not supply that gain. Sadly, many prayers today are also motivated by selfishness rather than holiness. People want something from God but ignore God's desires. Prayers expressed through holiness reflect both our desires and God's desires.

When we walk in holiness with God, we also open up the possibility of walking in holiness with people. As musical instruments must be in harmony with the same toning fork before being in tune with each other, holy relationships between people cannot work unless they first submit themselves in holiness to God. The human body also demonstrates this principle since body parts cannot coordinate with other parts except through their union with the head (brain). In the church body, we cannot relate to each other in true holiness except through our holy fellowship with Christ, who is the church's head. The apostle John expressed this principle very well in his first epistle.

> "For the life was manifested, and we have seen *it,* and bear witness, and show unto you that eternal life, which was with the Father and was manifested unto us. That which we have seen and heard declare we unto you, that ye also may have fellowship (holiness) with us: and truly our fellowship (holiness) *is* with the Father, and with his Son Jesus Christ....But if we walk in the light, as he is in the light, we have fellowship (holiness) one with another, and the blood of Jesus Christ his Son cleanseth us from all sin." (1Jn 1:2-3, 7 emphasis mine)

When we do not walk in holiness with God and others, we experience a significant lack of spiritual power in two ways. First, there is little or no ability to change from what we were before Christ to a "newness of life" in Christ (Rom 6:4). Paul states that although some people have a form of godliness –they are religious– they still go about their lives as lovers of their selves, covetous, boasters, proud, blasphemers, disobedient to parents, unthankful, unholy, without natural affection, trucebreakers, false accusers, incontinent (no self-control), fierce, despisers of those that are good, traitors, heady, high-minded, lovers of pleasures more than lovers of God. They do not change. Although personal spiritual change is not an overnight experience, and people are at different levels in their spiritual journey, according to John, where there is holiness with God and others, God will be free to cleanse us from sin (I John 1:9). That cleansing can *only* come about through the power of holiness, not through self-effort.

Secondly, there will be a lack of spiritual power to positively impact the world around us. As a result, we may feel we must resort to religious, social, political, or physical coercion to survive and achieve our goals. An example of this happened on January 6th, 2021, when people carrying Christian flags and signs joined with other militants in an attempt to force changes they felt necessary in the United States government. They did not take stock of Paul's words when he stated that we can "overcome evil with good" (Rom 12:21). God's admonishment to Joshua still applies to the church today. We must stand on "holy ground" for the best life possible.

God is saying in the story of Asa that when the church thinks it needs the support of worldly powers to succeed, those alliances may appear to solve the short-term problem but have long-term harmful consequences. When the church makes those alliances, it abandons and denies the power of holiness. Such was the case in 300 AD when the church endured great persecution and suffering. Constantine then made Christianity the state religion of the Roman Empire, which, at first glance, seemed to solve the church's problem. The persecution stopped. However, the church now had another problem. It could no longer function in holiness with God but now had to submit to the needs and desires of its new bed-fellow as well. When this happened, God backed out, and the church lost its power associated with holiness. We can look throughout history and find that Christians have never needed the support of a government to survive and thrive.

In some cases, Christians survived and were more vibrant under oppressive societies than when they had worldly governments to support them. Christianity was born and mushroomed during the rule of one of the most despotic regimes in the history of the world–the Roman Empire. When the Berlin Wall came down in 1989, they found that the churches in Communist East Berlin proved more spiritually vital than those in West Berlin, where they had governmental support. Also, Researchers from Boston University have found that, in the past Forty years, Christianity in China, under growing persecution, has grown faster than anywhere else in the world.[11]

When the United States' founding fathers established the Constitution as the primary law of the land, they knew full well the dangers of combining church and state. They had suffered under the state churches of Europe. Therefore, they took measures to ensure that the state had no authority to meddle with the free exercise of religion. They did not want the government to be able to force its will and control on the church in any way. However, since then, politicians have continually attempted to seduce the church into thinking they care about its spiritual agenda and that the church needs the government's support to succeed. Presidents have tried to entice spiritual leaders into their camps with state prayer meetings and invitations to give invocations and benedictions. In doing so, they sought a conservative religious base to enhance their political power, which worked beautifully. Men like Billy Graham and Jerry Falwell brought a huge conservative voter base into politics. In the process, Christians unconsciously began to think they could accomplish their agendas more effectively through political power, neglecting and denying the power of holiness. Today, a relatively large segment of the Christian Church has strayed so far to the political right that they have lost their sense of social responsibility and compassion and have marginalized people experiencing poverty and hardship, which is against the fundamental teachings of both the Old and New Testaments. Jesus said that if you do it unto the least of these, you do it unto him. People who ignore holiness with God will see no need to reach out in love to all humanity, seeking holy relationships with their neighbors.

It is time for Christians to realize that God ordained governments to maintain law and order and prevent chaos (Rom 13:1-7), but they have never been God's instrument of choice to improve people spiritually.

---

[11] Chalufour, Marc, "What's behind the Boom in Christianity in China", bu.edu, Feb 2, 2023

Instead, he has chosen the church to bless all humanity, operating in the power of holiness.

> "And in thy seed shall all the nations of the earth be blessed; because thou hast obeyed my voice." (Gen 22:18)

I am not saying that Christians should not participate in government. In our democracy, we have the freedom to vote our conscience and speak our minds, and we should exercise those freedoms. However, don't be deceived when politicians try to pass themselves off as spiritual when their fruits say otherwise. Wolves only dress in sheep's clothing to eat sheep, not bless them (Matt 7:15). By its very nature, the church must function as a counter-culture to the world's ways, and to do so, it must maintain its allegiance to God supremely (Acts:5:29). Paul speaks very clearly concerning our relationship with the world when He states:

> "Be ye not unequally yoked together with unbelievers: for what fellowship hath righteousness with unrighteousness? And what communion hath light with darkness? And what concord hath Christ with Belial? Or what part hath he that believeth with an infidel? And what agreement hath the temple of God with idols? For ye are the temple of the living God; as God hath said, I will dwell in them, and walk in *them;* and I will be their God, and they shall be my people. (2Co 6:14-16)

That's holiness! However, when we align with political forces for support rather than pursuing the power of holiness with God, the world will also perceive the church as aligned with that government's negative qualities.

Not all relationships are yoked relationships. To be yoked to someone or some organization is to say that you have obligated yourself to them somehow. For Christians, the only obligation or debt we have toward anyone is the debt of love. Paul states: "Owe no man anything, but to love one another: for he that loveth another hath fulfilled the law"

(Rom 13:8). When we yoke ourselves to and seek life through worldly sources–religious, social, political, or business– we have denied or neutralized the power of holiness to manage our lives. The Christian church must echo the testimony of Paul, who, while sitting in prison, could still exclaim, "I can do all things through Christ who strengthens me."

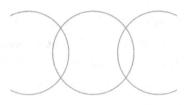

CHAPTER 12

THE DISCIPLINE OF HOLINESS

As I have said, God redeemed the Israelites from Egypt to make them a holy nation–a people set apart for Him.

> "Ye have seen what I did unto the Egyptians, and *how* I bore you on eagles' wings and brought you unto myself. Now, therefore, if ye will obey my voice indeed, and keep my covenant, then ye shall be a peculiar treasure unto me above all people: for all the earth *is* mine: And ye shall be unto me a kingdom of priests and a holy nation. These *are* the words which thou shalt speak unto the children of Israel" (Exo 19:4-6).

> "For thou *art* a holy people unto the LORD thy God, and the LORD hath chosen thee to be a special people unto himself, above all the nations that *are* upon the earth" (Deu 7: 6).

When I read these passages, I envision myself in a locker room where the coach is giving his team a motivational speech before the game. The coach tells the team that he picked each of them to be on the team because they are special and that if they do everything he taught them to do in practice, they will be a great team–even champions. The coach tells the team he has confidence in them and high expectations for them. Affirmation and expectation will powerfully motivate people to set lofty goals and practice the necessary discipline to achieve them.

Have you ever wondered what it means to be called "special" by God? I can understand that I am special to my wife, and she is special to me. But to be called special by the creator of the universe is pretty mind-blowing. Sadly, I have known many people who never received unique affirmations and, as a result, have never felt exceptional in any way. These people usually have very low self-esteem and set meager life standards. They are the people that end up living on the street, not because they are of inferior intellect or mentally ill, but because they have never been taught, disciplined, and encouraged to develop life skills. They may have received punishment for their misbehavior but found it easier to take punishment than to grow socially and spiritually. Affirming people is ultimately more powerful than punishment in encouraging people to improve their behavior.

High expectations are also crucial to a person's success. While working on my Master's degree in education administration, I saw some research the State of Michigan had done on the educational success of K-12 students. Researchers found a high correlation between the socioeconomic level of a family and their children's success in school. However, upon further examination of the deviations from that correlation (low socioeconomic/high success and high socioeconomic/low success), the researchers found that the family's socioeconomic level was not the determining success factor. Instead, the most accurate predictor of success was the level of expectations that parents and schools placed upon the students. Generally, those parents in high socioeconomic communities expected more of their children than those of low socioeconomic communities. However, the study showed that if parents' and teachers' expectations in a high socioeconomic community were low, their students' achievement levels were also low. Conversely, if the expectations of parents and teachers of low socioeconomic communities were high, their students tended to achieve at a high level.

We should be glad that God sets high expectations for his children.

In the Exodus passage quoted above, He states, "if ye will obey my voice indeed, and keep my covenant, then ye shall be a peculiar (special) treasure unto me above all people." This expectation is nothing short of holiness. Christ also affirms this high standard in the New Testament when He declares that "strait *is* the gate, and narrow *is* the way, which leads unto life, and few there be that find it" (Mat 7:14). Holiness was God's standard of expectation in the Old Testament and is God's standard in the New Testament. In the Old Testament, God used the Levitical Law to explain, in behavioral terms, how a holy Israel should live out their daily life. The fact that the word "holy" is mentioned 187 times in the Pentateuch and 94 times in the Levitical Law itself, I believe, confirms this. God also gave them judges to further guide the nation in holiness. However, as Israel became a monarchy, it moved away from the holiness principles articulated in the Law. They began to look to the monarchy for direction rather than God. Thus, God commissioned prophets to reprimand Israel for failing to live as a holy nation and to call them back into holiness. Such a message, however, didn't sit too well with the kings, so many prophets were persecuted and killed. In His introduction to his sermon on the mount, Jesus emphasized that His purpose was no different from the prophets' missions – to turn Israel back to holiness. He stressed that he was not eliminating the Levitical Law but clarifying and demonstrating it through His holy life.

> "Think not that I am come to destroy the law or the prophets: I am not come to destroy, but to fulfill" (Mat 5:17).

Although the Law and the prophets described and clarified the righteous life produced through holiness, they had no power to create righteousness in people. Moral behavior does not come about by imposing rules and control from the outside but by transforming the inner man through a holy relationship with God. Only Christ can renew hearts and return them to a holy union with God through His death and resurrection. His atoning work tore open the veil of guilt that separates people from God (2 Cor 3:1, 4). Then He sent His Holy Spirit to indwell His children and, through holiness, discipline them in righteousness (Rom

8:4). In His high priestly prayer recorded in John 17, Jesus stated he desired to make holy or sanctify those who received Him (Joh 17:19). Paul tells us that we should yield our members as servants to righteousness unto holiness (Rom 6:19). It is statements like these that indicate to me that holiness, not righteousness, is and always has been the primary theme of the Bible. Without holiness, we will not see God (Heb 12:14). If holiness is God's immediate desire for us, then our goal in life must be holiness. We must have a commitment to living in unity with God and with the children of God.

There are two main functions of holiness in our lives. Its first function is to become the disciplining force in our lives. It is our intimacy with God that, through the Holy Spirit's discipline, produces righteousness in our lives. When we are willing to walk in the Spirit and give Him total control of our life's activities, He will be free to guide us in righteousness. Paul says that it is not enough to live in the Spirit. We must allow the Spirit to control or discipline our walk – "If we live in the Spirit, let us also walk in the Spirit" (Gal 5:25). Through disciplining our walk, the Spirit produces the various fruits of righteousness in our lives.

> "But the fruit of the Spirit is love, joy, peace, longsuffering, gentleness, goodness, faith, meekness, temperance: against such there is no law" (Gal 5:22,23).

God introduced the "Sabbath" in the Old Testament to celebrate and facilitate holiness in His people. He commanded the Israelites to set the seventh day of the week aside to rest from their labors and commune with God. God would use this intimate time to guide their walk and put them on the right path to success. Isaiah explains it this way:

> "If thou turn away thy foot from (*because of*) the sabbath, *from* doing thy pleasure on my holy day; and call the sabbath a delight, the holy of the LORD, honourable; and shalt honour him, not doing thine own ways, nor finding thine own pleasure, nor speaking *thine own* words: Then shalt thou delight thyself in the LORD,

and I will cause thee to ride upon the high places of
the earth, and feed thee with the heritage of Jacob, thy
father: for the mouth of the LORD hath spoken *it"* (Isa
58:13, 14 emphasis mine).

God called this a holy day because He desired that Israel set it apart
for Him. On the Sabbath, Israel was to cease their work -- and even
their obsessive mental preoccupation with work -- so that they might
experience the new and restorative power of holiness. Isaiah said this
celebration of holiness would put them on the "high road"– the road
of righteousness and success. When we delight in observing a time of
sabbath as an exercise of holiness with God, we, through the Holy Spirit,
will see the fruits of righteousness appearing in our lives.

The second function of holiness is a result of the first. According to
Christ in His High-priestly prayer, holiness validates to the world that
God did indeed send His Son to this earth.

"That they all may be one; as thou, Father, *art* in me,
and I in thee, that they also may be one in us: that the
world may believe that thou hast sent me." (Joh 17:21)

Until the world can see that expression of holiness and its benefits
in the Church that it cannot find outside the Church, it will never take
the message of Christ seriously. Holiness produces righteousness, while
a lack of holiness produces hypocrites. Hypocrites talk the talk but do
not walk the walk. Therefore, they are not worthy witnesses of Christ
because they have never had their walk disciplined by holiness. (Eph 4:1)
Those early Christians began to elevate certain men to an unacceptable
level of leadership in their lives–preferring one over the other– rather
than seeing them as men God had given the Church to unify it, not to
disrupt the unity and holiness of the Church.

"And he gave some, apostles; and some, prophets; and
some, evangelists; and some, pastors and teachers; For
the perfecting of the saints, for the work of the ministry,

for the edifying of the body of Christ: Till we all come in the unity of the faith, and of the knowledge of the Son of God, unto a perfect man, unto the measure of the stature of the fulness of Christ: That we *henceforth* be no more children, tossed to and fro, and carried about with every wind of doctrine, by the sleight of men, *and* cunning craftiness, whereby they lie in wait to deceive; But speaking the truth in love, may grow up into him in all things, which is the head, *even* Christ: From whom the whole body fitly joined together and compacted by that which every joint supplieth, according to the effectual working in the measure of every part, maketh increase of the body unto the edifying of itself in love." (Eph 4:11-16)

"Now this I say, that every one of you saith, I am of Paul; and I of Apollos; and I of Cephas; and I of Christ. (I Co 1:12)

"For while one saith, I am of Paul; and another, I *am* of Apollos; are ye not carnal"? (1Co 3:4)

In the second chapter of I John, the apostle John also warns the Church that there will be unworthy leaders he calls "anti-Christs" in the latter days. These people were originally part of the Church but left it to start a following that would promote and perpetuate their values above and beyond those of Christ. They were anti-Christ in the sense that they were trying to build their kingdoms rather than the kingdom of God. This anti-Christ mentality has been present in the Church throughout history and is very active today. Many churches and para-Church organizations operate under the banner of Christianity but promote their agendas rather than holiness and the Kingdom of God. A.W. Tozer sums it up quite well when he says:

"The grosser manifestations of these sins, egotism, exhibitionism, and self-promotion, are strangely tolerated in

Christian leaders, even in circles of impeccable orthodoxy. They are so much in evidence as actually, for many people, to become identified with the gospel. I trust it is not a cynical observation to say that they appear these days to be a requisite for popularity in some sections of the Church visible. Promoting self under the guise of promoting Christ is currently so common as to excite little notice."[12]

It appears that the devil has succeeded quite well in minimizing the impact of the Church on the world from its inception until today simply by causing division and separation in the Church. He has done it by promoting men and women to the level that rightly belongs to the Holy Spirit– that of spiritual discipline. Instead of allowing only holiness with God to be our discipliner, the Church searches worldwide for charismatic, intellectual, forceful, and self-promoting leaders – even politicians – to give them the illusion of power. True spiritual power can only be found under the discipline of the Holy Spirit through holiness. John says that if we have a holy relationship (an anointing) with the Holy Spirit, we don't need Christian leaders to take charge of the spiritual discipline in our lives.

> "These *things* have I written unto you concerning them that seduce you. But the anointing which ye have received of him abideth in you, and ye need not that any man teach you: but as the same anointing teacheth you of all things, and is truth, and is no lie, and even as it hath taught you, ye shall abide in him." (1Jn 2:26-27)

We must ask then, "What is the task of the five-fold ministries expounded in Ephesians four?"

The work of those ministries is to introduce people to and guide them into a holy relationship with God– and then step back. However, because most Christian leaders do not have a working definition of holiness (oneness with God), they do not know where their job ends.

---

[12] Tozer, A. W. (Aiden Wilson). The Pursuit of God (p. 22). Kindle Edition.

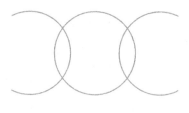

CHAPTER 13

THE FIRE OF HOLINESS

Speaking of holiness as having a fiery quality may seem unusual because we usually associate fire with destruction. However, the Bible often portrays God as fire and as smoke. Therefore, it would follow that a holy relationship with God could also have a fiery quality. In this chapter, I will explore how a holy relationship with God can both purify and empower our lives.

We may ask why God displayed Himself to early humans as a fire. It may have something to do with how early humans viewed the world. In ancient times, people perceived the world to consist of four elements: air (gases), water (liquids), earth (solids), and fire. It was a kind of three-plus-one mentality where fire was considered an element of change because it could affect change in the other three. Portraying Himself as either air, water, or earth would imply to early man that He was a physical god like the idols humans created from stone, wood, and various metals. However, "God is a spirit" (Jn 4:24), and, as a spirit, He has the power to change things, as does fire. Because of that, He manifested Himself as fire many times, especially in the Old Testament. Below are a few biblical references in which God showed Himself as fire.

The first incident which portrays God as fire is found in Genesis, where God made a covenant with Abram (Gen 15:17). Next, there was the fiery bush (Ex 3:2), the pillar of fire and smoke (Ex 13:21,22), the mountain of smoke and fire (Ex 19:18), the altar in the Tabernacle (Lev

9:24), the Mount Carmel sacrifice (I Kings 18:38), the Holy Spirit (Mark 9:49; Luke 3:16; Acts 2:3; I Thes 5:19), the judgment of fire (I Cor 3:13), and the discipline of God (Heb 12:29; Rev 3:18,19).

The Covenants of Fire

There are three occasions in the Bible where fiery manifestations appeared as part of a covenant ceremony. You may ask why God begins His relationships with a covenant. I would answer that God only concerns Himself with holy relationships, not casual ones. Holy relationships are formed to bring two or more beings into an intimate relationship of oneness, characterized by complete unity of purpose, reciprocal faith, love, purity, and naked transparency. This kind of relationship must begin with commitment. You cannot initiate this relationship with a "shot in the dark" mentality. By this, I mean a relationship that says, "Well, let's try it and see what happens. We can always break it off again if it doesn't work." Such a relationship allows circumstances to determine the outcome of the relationship. Only through a covenant that supersedes events can one hope to establish a holy relationship. In the case of marriages, couples supposedly covenant themselves to holiness (for better or worse, for richer or poorer, in sickness and health, till death do us part). Still, under pressure, they often renege on those promises and let circumstances determine their future rather than their promises. However, God does not renege on His promises. He will always honor His commitment to holiness—as we have seen in the book of Isaiah (Chapter 8)—unless we willfully deny our commitment to Him. God will not force holiness upon us. He wants us to enter and maintain that relationship with Him through free will. Therefore, He does not interfere with our choice if we renounce our commitment to holiness.

> "If we suffer, we shall also reign with *him:* if we deny
> *him,* he also will deny us:
>   If we believe not, *yet* he abideth faithful: he cannot
> deny himself." (2Ti 2:12,13)

I am concerned about those who teach a form of eternal security that says we can never lose our salvation once we commit to God. I agree that no sin or lack of faith will cause us to lose our relationship with God. However, a deliberate choice on our part to turn away from God will force God to release us if He is to respect our free will.

> "For *it is* impossible for those who were once enlightened, and have tasted of the heavenly gift, and were made partakers of the Holy Ghost, and have tasted the good word of God, and the powers of the world to come, If they shall fall away, to renew them again unto repentance; seeing they crucify to themselves the Son of God afresh, and put *him* to an open shame." (Heb 6:4-6)

We must remember that God is not looking for perfect people. By this, I mean people who have met God's standard of righteousness, of which there are none. He is looking for a thief on the cross who asks, "Would you remember me when you come into your kingdom?" He's looking for a woman at the well who has struggled in her relationships with men. He is looking for imperfect people whom He can restore through holiness. He's looking for people who genuinely desire an intimate relationship with Him. In other words, He is looking for holiness, not righteousness. That holiness will produce righteousness.

The first covenant between God and man appears in Genesis chapter 15, where God makes a covenant with Abram. God had told Abram that He would give him a land to possess (Gen 12: 1; 13:15,17), a family legacy of uncountable seed (Gen 12:2; 13:16, 15.5), and unfailing protection (Gen 12:3; 15:1), but Abram still had some doubts. Abram was not unlike any of us who, even though we want to believe in God, also reacted to God's promises with skepticism. I must say that God does not expect us to have great faith immediately, just *some* faith–enough to cause them to act. He will take even mustard seed faith (Luke 17: 6)and count it as righteousness (Gen 15:6).

Having received Abram's "seed faith," God now covenanted to follow through on His promises to Abram. He told Abram to lay out three

animals and two birds as sacrifices. Abram was to split the three animals
in half and lay the halves on the ground opposite each other. He was then
told not to split the birds in half but to lay them opposite each other on
the ground. What was God doing here? I believe God was asking Abram
to validate his small amount of faith in Him through some action before
He could proceed with the covenant. We know that the apostle James
declares that one's actions confirm one's faith (James 2). Paul says that a
reasonable proof of our faith in God is to present our bodies as "a living
sacrifice" (Rom 12:1). I believe God declares that His valid promises are
contingent on a faith validated by action—no matter how much.

Once Abram completed the presentation of his sacrifice, he worked
all day, keeping the scavenger birds from eating the sacrifices. By night-
fall, he may have wondered whether God would receive his sacrifice and
culminate the covenant ritual. He finally fell into a deep sleep, which the
Bible describes as a "horror of great darkness." It may have been caused
by fatigue or emotional exhaustion; we don't know. Once Abram fell
asleep, he could not argue or debate with God concerning God's promise, and God was free to fulfill His covenant with him. The story states
that God told Abram (in what I believe was a vision or a dream) that he
would have a great family, but they would go through 400 years of hardship and persecution (Egypt) before inheriting the promised land. Then,
God caused a smoking furnace and a burning lamp to pass between the
sacrifices, signifying God's presence, and validation of His promise.

The burning lamp, often used in mid-eastern covenants, represents
God's words that give us enlightenment, guidance, admonishment, re-
buke, and revelation. Consider the following scriptures.

"Thy word is a lamp unto my feet, and a light unto my
path."(Psa 119:105)

"*Is* not my word like as a fire? saith the LORD…?"
(Jer 23:29)

"Out of his mouth go burning lamps, *and* sparks of fire
leap out." (Job 41:19)

"There went up a smoke out of his nostrils, and fire out of his mouth…." (Psa 18:8)

"wherefore thus saith the LORD God of hosts, Because ye speak this word, behold, I will make my words in thy mouth fire…" (Jer 5:14)

The fiery manifestation of God's words became very dominant at Mount Sinai, where God instituted His second covenant with humans, known to Christians as the "Old Covenant," or the Torah. In the Old Covenant, the Israelites were required to obey God and keep the law, and in return, He would protect and bless them (Duet 30:15-18; I Sam 12:14-15). The anniversary of this event became known as the "Feast of Weeks," the "Feast of Harvest," "Pentecost," or "Shavu'ot." It was celebrated fifty days after the Passover when the Israelites believed God stepped out of heaven and into the mount, appearing as thunder, lightning, smoke, and fire. They were so terrified that they asked God not to speak to them directly but through Moses. The English version of the Sinai account uses thunder and lightning to indicate the delivery of the words of God (Ex 20:18). However, the Hebrew version of this verse says, "They saw the voices and the torches."[13] But how do you see voices? One ancient Jewish tradition states that when God spoke, sparks or tiny torches shot out of the fire and encircled the whole camp before resting on each person.[14] In Job, that idea is also expressed when it states, "Out of his mouth go burning lamps, *and* sparks of fire leap out" (Job 41:19). Another piece of Jewish folklore claims that the people at Sinai saw the voices and heard them in many different languages.[15] No wonder they were terrified at God's voice.

In Acts 2:3, We find the third covenant of fire. This covenant is called the new covenant by Christians. Jesus prophesied this covenant in the gospel of John, chapters 14-16, as the coming of His Holy Spirit

[13] What was the Old Covenant?, gotquestions.org
[14] Weissman, Moshe. *The Midrash Says, Shemos*, Bnai Yaakov Publicasions. (1995), page 182 citing Midrash Chazut
[15] Eg Shemot Rabbah 5:9 from D. ThomasLancaster(www.ffoz.org)May16,2021

to dwell in His followers and speak for Him. The Spirits' mission to the followers of Christ was threefold–1) to lead them in all truth, 2) to show them things to come, and 3) to show them everything they would inherit in Christ (John 16: 13-15).

In the old covenant, God told Israel to kill a perfect lamb and spread its blood on the doorpost of their home to protect them from the impending judgment of Eygpt. However, God provided the lamb (Jesus) in the new covenant and applied His blood to the Church, thus protecting it from the impending judgment of the world.

After His resurrection and before He ascended to Heaven, Jesus told His followers to wait in Jerusalem for God to send the Holy Ghost to confirm the new covenant. Interestingly, that confirmation came fifty days after Passover, the same as the confirmation of the Old Covenant.

> "And, being assembled together with *them,* commanded them that they should not depart from Jerusalem, but wait for the promise of the Father, which, *saith he,* ye have heard of me." (Act 1:4)

God had something big planned. He was setting the stage for the birth of the Church. When Pentecost came, the disciples were praying together, Jerusalem was crowded with Jews from all over the then-known world, and God moved.

> "And suddenly there came a sound from heaven like a mighty rushing wind, and it filled the house where they were sitting. And there appeared unto them cloven tongues like as of fire, and it sat upon each of them. And they were all filled with the Holy Ghost, and began to speak with other tongues, as the Spirit gave them utterance." (Act 2:2-4)

To gentiles, these activities of Pentecost, or Shavu'ot, may seem strange or even a bit unrealistic. However, to the Jews versed in Jewish history and tradition, those activities not only repeated that first Shavu'ot at Sinai but spoke to the strong continuity between Judaism/Torah and the church – not an opposition. Is it any wonder that three thousand souls recognized this as a work of Yahweh and placed their trust in Christ as their Messiah? (Acts 2:41)

The Refining Fire

In two of the three occasions of the covenant fire of God, He portrays Himself as fire and smoke. I believe each depicts different but related features of God when dealing with His people. I've stated before that fire represents God's words. The smoke, however, would indicate that the fire was also burning something. The Bible says that God is a consuming God. (Deut 4:24, 9:3, Heb 12:29) I believe the smoke symbolizes all the things in our lives that are useless and spiritually impure, things that hinder the empowerment of the Holy Spirit, and things that are self-initiated rather than God-initiated. Isaiah states:

> "Therefore as the fire devoureth the stubble, and the flame consumeth the chaff, *so* their root shall be as rottenness, and their blossom shall go up as dust: because they have cast away the law of the LORD of hosts, and despised the word of the Holy One of Israel." (Isa 5:24)

Paul also warns the Corinthian Church that they can expect that God will judge the works they build on the foundation of Christ.

> "For other foundation, can no man lay than that is laid, which is Jesus Christ. Now if any man build upon this foundation gold, silver, precious stones, wood, hay, stubble; every man's work shall be made manifest: for the day shall declare it, because it shall be revealed by fire; and the fire shall try every man's work of what sort it is. If any man's work abide which he hath built thereupon, he shall receive a reward. If any man's work shall

be burned, he shall suffer loss: but he himself shall be
saved; yet so as by fire." (I Cor 3:11-15)

The principle in these scriptures is that anything that is not of God,
or any work that God does not initiate, will ultimately be consumed
by God because they are blemishes on His Church. (Eph 5: 27) That
sounds harsh. However, God has a stringent standard for what can be
considered spiritual work. It is not the work I do for God that is spiritual.
It is the work that God does through me. Even our love for others must
be channeled through God. Paul says in Ephesians 5, verse 2 that we
must love as Christ loved and give ourselves an offering and sacrifice *to*
God *for* others. God must be the source and the guidance of our love
for others. We cannot love others as we should and must allow God to
love others through us. We are just vehicles of His love, not the source.
As I said in chapter three, we are just "old hoses." There are activities in
both the world and the Church that appear to be good works and are
supported by people. However, that does not mean that they are spiritual
works having spiritual value with God. To meet God's standard of what
is spiritual, it must pass the following criteria: 1) God must initiate it.
2) God must empower it. And 3) God must get the glory. "For of him,
and through him, and to him, *are* all things: to whom *be* glory forever.
Amen." (Rom 11:36)

The refining fire of God is the disciplining voice of God. Its primary
goal is to remove all things that blemish our spiritual beauty. Paul explains this process in Ephesians Five.

> "That he might sanctify and cleanse it (the Church)
> with the washing of water by the word, That he might
> present it to himself a glorious church, not having spot,
> or wrinkle, or any such thing; but that it should be holy
> and without blemish." (Eph 5:26-27 emphasis mine)

George MacDonald explains this process this way.

"For love loves unto purity. Love has ever in view the absolute loveliness of that which it beholds. Where loveliness is incomplete, and love cannot love its fill of loving, it spends itself to make more lovely, that it may love more; it strives for perfection, even that itself may be perfected—not in itself, but in the object…. Therefore all that is not beautiful in the beloved, all that comes between and is not of love's kind, must be destroyed. And our God is a consuming fire."[16]

I would add that we allow God to cleanse and purify us through His word only in an atmosphere of holiness.

The Empowering Fire

The second goal of God's refining fire is to prepare us for the empowering fire of the Holy Spirit, which is God's ultimate goal for us.

"But ye shall receive power, after that the Holy Ghost is come upon you: and ye shall be witnesses unto me both in Jerusalem, and in all Judaea, and in Samaria, and unto the uttermost part of the earth." (Act 1:8)

What sets the new covenant in Acts 2 apart from the Abrahamic and Sinai covenants is that there is no smoke, just fire. Therefore, one must conclude that the Holy Spirit's function in that context was empowering rather than refining. This is not to say Christians do not need refining in their Christian lives. However, I would suggest that refining is not the primary job of the Holy Ghost. In the Gospel of John, Christ taught that the role of the Holy Spirit was to 1) lead us in all truth, 2) show us things to come, and 3) show us what all we have at our disposal through Christ (John 16:13-15). All these functions are empowering, not refining.

According to Hebrews 12, our Father-God reserves the refining or

---

[16] Lewis, C. S.. George MacDonald . HarperCollins. Kindle Edition.

chastening role I discussed in the previous section for Himself through His word and experiences.

> "If ye endure chastening, God dealeth with you as with sons; for what son is he whom the Father chasteneth not? But if ye be without chastisement, whereof all are partakers, then are ye bastards, and not sons. Furthermore, we have had fathers of our flesh which corrected *us,* and we gave *them* reverence: shall we not much rather be in subjection unto the Father of spirits and live"? (Heb 12:7-9)

As I have stated, I believe God's discipline or chastening prepares us for the empowerment of the Holy Spirit. As the chastening of God cleanses us from sins, attitudes, and belief systems that hinder our spiritual vision of God, the Holy Spirit is free to take over and empower our lives for spiritual victory. In chapter eleven, I made the point that churches under persecution have grown and prospered much more than the churches where there is no persecution. In chapter twelve, I made the point that expectations are the foundation of all successes and that God has high expectations of his children; therefore, He must discipline us like a coach who wants his team to win. God expects us not just to be Bible scholars with extensive scripture knowledge. He expects that we have spiritual victories over the flesh, the world, and the devil; to do that, we must face and overcome the enemy.

The most potent example of a human overcoming Satan appears in the story of Job. God challenged Satan to a battle with His man Job. He didn't do this to punish Job but to prove to the devil that a person committed to holiness is unconquerable. Few, if any, of us will go through what Job went through, but God will allow persecution, which He believes will strengthen us, not destroy us.

> "There hath no temptation taken you but such as is common to man: but God *is* faithful, who will not suffer you to be tempted above that ye are able; but will

with the temptation also make a way to escape, that ye
may be able to bear *it*" (1Cor 10:13).

Those victories over the world, the flesh, and the devil show us that
Christians who walk in holiness are winners, not losers. This victorious
life is what Acts 1: 8 is speaking of when it says that the Holy Spirit em-
powers us to be witnesses. Many Christians believe it is the Holy Spirit's
job to give us the boldness to speak on Christ's behalf. That may be true
to a certain extent, but I don't think Christ is asking us to be His "super
salespeople." People who try to sell Christianity tend to turn me off.
They like to argue theology and have a superior- rather Pharisaical- air.
Looking at their lifestyles, I see nothing that would make me want their
kind of life. Many of them can be very overbearing and threatening. The
trump card in their sales pitch seems to be the "fear of hell."

However, Christian witnesses testify to what they have experienced
or seen, presenting the Christian life as a life of power and joy, not a fire
escape. That testimony doesn't need to be laced with a lot of theology.
An example of this is recorded in the gospel of John, chapter nine, where
Jesus encounters a blind man. The disciples asked Christ if the man was
blind because of some sin on his or his parents' part. Christ's answer
makes the point that I'm attempting to make.

"Jesus answered, Neither hath this man sinned, nor
his parents: but that the works of God should be made
manifest in him." (John 9:3)

Jesus was not trying to make a theologian of the blind man but a
witness. When the Pharisees caught up with the man, they tried to run
his experience through their theological meat grinder. They attacked
him and his parents because they had no theological answer for what
had happened. All the man could say was, "One thing I know, that,
whereas I was blind, now I see" (John 9:25). That is the primary goal
of the Holy Spirit–to manifest the supernatural power of God in us as
He did in Christ. We then are to show and tell what God has done or is
doing in our lives. We don't have to explain it; we only give witness to

it. I heard a pastor express this phenomenon very simply but powerfully. He said, "We may not have a polished theology to share, but we all need a story to share."

Sadly, few stories in the Christian Church today would convince believers and non-believers alike that Christianity has something more powerful to offer them than what they have heard in the Church. Most evangelism and teaching have utilized guilt and the fear of hell as the mainstay of their program. I accepted Christ into my heart as a thirteen-year-old lad out of fear but never heard a witness to the abundant power of God until I was twenty-two. At a weekend men's retreat, the camp director did not preach per se but told his story of how God miraculously gave him this beautiful camp and maintained it for him. To share those stories would take another book; fortunately, there is a book entitled "BARAKEL, God's Miracle."

That weekend, God opened my eyes to see that He was trying to do something in my life that was different from the Christian life I had heard about in Church. It resonated with my Spirit and confirmed what I had experienced during college and after. I realized that the Holy Spirit miraculously changed the direction of my life from a farm boy/butcher to a college chemistry major to a teacher in four short years. Though I assumed that my course was set and that I would be a science teacher for the rest of my life, that was not the case. I didn't realize that God wasn't finished yet.

First, God closed off all my romantic endeavors to find a wife and gave me the wife of His choosing. She told me that God told her I was the man she would marry. Fifty-seven years later, I can only say, "Thank you, God." Then, while teaching, I encountered a strange problem I had never expected to face. Students began to ask me spiritual questions, and I spent much class time answering and discussing those questions. I felt guilty because, as important as those matters were, I was getting paid to teach science. I finally asked God to help find a way for me to relate to these young people as individuals, not students. He did just that.

In the third year of teaching, the middle school principal retired. I wondered, could this be God's answer to my request? To find out, I wrote a letter of application to the superintendent saying I would like the job and that if given the job, I would get a master's degree in education administration. A few weeks later, the superintendent approached me and said, "You got the job." Wow, that was easy, but how did that happen without any discussion or interview with the Board of Education? That question was answered later when a board member asked me if I wanted to know how it happened. He then told me the superintendent told the board that he wanted to hire me because of my Christian values and the board voted to approve his request. All I could think of was God's comment to the Church of Philadelphia in the third chapter of Revelations– "I know thy works: behold, I have set before thee an open door, and no man can shut it: for thou hast a little strength, and hast kept my word, and hast not denied my name" (Rev 3:8).

Giving me an administrative position in the school was the final phase of God's training program to fulfill His vision for me. I remember sitting in my new office at the ripe old age of twenty-four and thinking, "Wow, I'm the boss." I had no idea what was coming. I started introducing new innovative ideas, which never worked because I had no idea how to implement them. I thought I only had to "bark," and my teachers would jump. After a few years of playing that game, my teachers got tired and started complaining to people who would listen, and unbeknown to me, people got on the school board with one objective–to get rid of me.

Two things happened that saved my job. First was a female teacher who dared to confront me directly and tell me everything I was doing wrong. I had no idea. Next, God gave me a vision of myself seated atop a pyramid. Under me were my teachers, and under them were the students. My first impulse was to say, "Yes, that looks right to me. I am the boss, the teachers are under my authority, and the students are under their jurisdiction." Then God shocked me by saying, "Turn the pyramid upside down. You are there to serve and support your teachers, and they are there to help their students."

It was those two experiences that finally transformed me into an acceptable administrator. As I matured in my job, I couldn't help thinking I had arrived. People began to affirm my abilities as an administrator.

Therefore, I wrongly concluded that education administration was God's plan for my life, and I began to explore all the possibilities of advancement in that profession. However, God had other plans. He shut all of the vocational doors I explored. Then in 1973, something happened that confirmed that God's vocation for me was not in education but in Christian ministry, and every change up to that point-including summer construction work- was to give me the skills I needed to pastor a church-not just any church but the particular church I was attending.

In the spring of that year, I made a youthful mistake and publicly "rebuked" an elder of the church. The whole church turned against me and, in the annual business meeting, voted me out of every job I had in the church. I was angry and frustrated. I considered leaving, but God had a better plan. That summer, I volunteered to help in a summer camping program in the wilderness of Canada. I had to think about my future in the church I had attended for nine years. One morning, about five o'clock, I sat on a rock by a wilderness lake, reading John chapter six, where Christ described Himself as the bread of life. Suddenly, I heard a voice saying, "You're feeding at the wrong source. I'll feed you, and you feed them." I looked around to see who said it, but there was nobody but me out there. It had to be God. I understood what the first statement meant–I was feeding off people and not God. However, the second statement baffled me. Three months later, I got the explanation.

That fall, the church's pastor decided to leave and start a new church whose sole mission was to support the Christian school of which he was superintendent. At his going-away dinner, He suddenly stood and called an impromptu business meeting. The agenda was to vote me in as interim pastor of the church. That action somewhat blindsided my wife and me. She because she had never planned on being a pastor's wife, and me because I would never have guessed that the people who voted me out of every office in the church six months before would vote me in as pastor now–but they did. Sometime later, they upgraded me to part-time, and seven years later, after the church had grown to close to two hundred people, I resigned from the school and became a full-time pastor. This has become my story! When I doubt God, I only must recall my story, and my faith is restored. I have also had many opportunities to share my story with those who needed encouragement in their spiritual journey.

When I was working as an educator, an older gentleman came to me and exclaimed, "I have three sons who have gone through the school system, and I have been watching you. There is something different about you, and I would like to know what it is." As a result of his observation, I led him to a relationship with Christ. A month later, he died of a heart attack. The truth is that many people are looking for someone to show them a better life than they presently have. Unless we witness a Spirit-empowered life, they could miss out on the life God desires for them.

So why is holiness so crucial to a victorious Christian life? The closer we live to the fire (the voice of God), the more significant the fire's effect on our lives. Holiness, or being in total unity and harmony with God, will confirm His covenant with us and refine and empower our lives to bring glory to God.

A quote from George MacDonald typifies my transition between the refining/disciplining fire of God and the empowering fire of the Holy Spirit.

"[3] Divine Burning:

He will shake heaven and earth, that only the unshakable may remain: he is a consuming fire, that only that which cannot be consumed may stand forth eternal. It is the nature of God, so terribly pure that it destroys all that is not pure as fire, which demands like purity in our worship. He will have purity. It is not that the fire will burn us if we do not worship thus; yea, will go on burning within us after all that is foreign to it has yielded to its force, no longer with pain and consuming, but as the highest consciousness of life, the presence of God.[17]

---

[17] Lewis, C. S.. George MacDonald . HarperCollins. Kindle Edition.

Only as we allow the fire of God to purge that which fogs our vision or awareness of God's presence can we begin to see God as He is—an ever-present God of purity and great power. Then we will proclaim as Job did: "I have heard of thee by the hearing of the ear, but now mine eye seeth thee. Wherefore I abhor myself, and repent in dust and ashes" (Job 42:5, 6).

The difference between theology and reality is the difference between hearing about God and seeing the presence of God in our lives. It is the difference between having knowledge about God and experiencing the power of God. When the woman at the well asked Jesus where she should worship (a religious question), He responded with a spiritual answer, "We must worship Him in Spirit and truth (reality). It is not where we worship God but how we worship God that makes a difference in our lives. Religion and theology can be helpful, but they are not the end; they are only a means to the end. The end is holiness and its transforming effect on our lives.

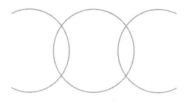

CHAPTER 14

THE PEACE OF HOLINESS

"Glory to God in the highest, and on earth peace, good will toward men." (Luk 2:14)

"Follow peace with all *men,* and holiness, without which no man shall see the Lord." (Heb 12:14)

Peace is the most sought-after state of mind or level of consciousness on earth. People at peace with God, at peace with themselves, and at peace with others tend to live in a state of bliss and have a powerful influence on the world around them. When I think of this kind of peace, I think of Jesus asleep in the back of the boat during a violent storm while his disciples panicked. They woke Him and said, "Don't you care that we perish?" Mark says that Jesus stood up, rebuked the wind, and told the sea to be calm. Then he turned to His disciples and said, "Why are you afraid? Where is your faith?" Can you imagine these men looking at each other and asking, "What kind of guy is this that can speak to and control the weather?" It is almost humorous. The answer to their question is not that Jesus was God—though He was. According to Paul in his letter to the Philippians, Jesus laid aside His Godhead. Therefore, He did not do this as God but as a man walking in perfect holiness with God— the same privilege we have when we walk in absolute holiness with God.

Jesus claimed that those who believed in Him would do the things He did (Jn 14:12).

The possibility of peace allowing you to have total rest during a storm and having the power to command the wind will sound ludicrous to the world and most Christians. Why, then, did Paul say in Romans eight that the creation, or nature, was waiting for the manifestation of the sons of God?

> "For the earnest expectation of the creature waiteth for the manifestation of the sons of God. For the creature was made subject to vanity, not willingly, but by reason of him who hath subjected *the same* in hope. Because the creature itself also shall be delivered from the bondage of corruption into the glorious liberty of the children of God. For we know that the whole creation groaneth and travaileth in pain together until now." (Rom 8:19-22)

I will be the first to say I have yet to reach the point of holiness where I can command nature, whether it be storms or Mountains. Neither were the disciples at that point. However, I will say, as Paul said. "I have not arrived, but I am "pressing on" for the mark."

Our lack of peace has much to do with our feelings of helplessness and separation concerning the world around us. We are not in charge of nature and, therefore, feel like pawns. Such was not the case in the Garden of Eden and, according to Paul, will not be the case in the future. Then nature will be delivered "*into* the glorious liberty of the children of God." Man will again be in charge, as in the garden.

Before going on, I must clarify what I mean by peace. In the Bible, there are two fundamental types of peace. One is to "hold one's peace," which means to remain silent. The other is a state of tranquility, bliss, and safety. It is this second concept of peace that I want to dwell on. In Hebrew, the word for this peace is "shalom." It means peace, harmony, wholeness, completeness, prosperity, welfare, and tranquility. In the Greek language, it is the word "eirēnē" (*i-rah'-nay*), from a primary verb, "eirō," meaning to join or to set at one again. We can see from these definitions that peace results when two entities reconcile and come together in unity and harmony, which is holiness.

Three separations cause a lack of peace in the world. They are separation from God, separation from oneself, and separation from other people. The first of these separations happened in the Garden of Eden. There, Adam and Eve chose to guide their lives through the knowledge of good and evil (a moral conscience) rather than by a holy walk with God. Therefore, God, respecting their free will, did not stop them but warned that their preference to walk that way would kill them and that they could no longer live in the garden. Unfortunately, through that separation, the Edenic couple lost their ability to control their world with the spoken word as Jesus did in the boat; they now had to manage it through hard physical labor and the sweat of their brows. The only good news in this story is that God, being holy, immediately promised a way in which people can regain a holy relationship with Him if they so choose (Gen 3:15). I would emphasize that humanity lost its divine relationship with God by choice and still does today. Therefore, we must regain it by choosing to accept the atoning work of Christ as God's way back to holiness.

As a result of Adam's separation from God in the garden, he also found himself separated from himself. He was now caught between what he knew to be correct according to his conscience and what his self-nature or ego, now divorced from God, preferred to do. His alienation from God resulted in self-alienation. Nothing is more devastating to a person than being divided, knowing the right thing to do but not wanting or being able to do it. Paul expresses this dilemma in Romans, chapter 7, where he sums up the situation by exclaiming, "Oh wretched man that I am." Such a struggle within a person can and eventually will cause that person to develop a hatred for themselves and a desire to punish or destroy oneself. Self-punishment usually takes the form of adopting a destructive lifestyle or an unconscious desire to get sick. It can also cause a person to become depressed. The ultimate form of self-punishment is suicide– which is becoming an epidemic, especially among teenagers today.

The third separation is separation from other people. While walking in holiness with Eve in the garden, Adam described her as "bone of his bone and flesh of his flesh." However, after the fall, he referred to her as "that woman." What happened? Adam and Eve lost their unity with God, and it quickly followed that they lost their unity with each other. When Adam and Eve were united in their submission to each other and God in holiness, their primary concern was always, "What is God's will?" After the fall or separation, their mindset became, "What do I want?" Furthermore, because of his separation from God and his wife, Adam readily blamed Eve and God for his choice to eat the fruit– "that woman You gave me."

All the world's strife today results from one or more of the above separations. It is somehow inherent in the idea of separation that one must compete and fight to be happy, whether it be a football game or a war. The concept of holiness is almost non-existent in the practical ways we live; therefore, peace on earth is also almost non-existent. We have relegated holiness to an ethereal religious realm so that no one comprehends what it means. Thus, the world makes fun of the term and uses it to describe everything from cows to smoke. By observing this separation in the world, science has concluded that society advances based on the "survival of the fittest." This observation justifies the evolutionistic mindset that wars and conflict are needed for society to progress; therefore, we should accept such conflict as a necessary part of life. As a result, the world has developed a tribal mentality. It is your tribe against my tribe. Even in the Christian church, we have divided ourselves into denominations based on minute theological differences that have little to do with the central theme of Christianity, which Paul describes as "Christ and Him crucified" (I Cor 2:1-2).

If we are going to undo this separatist mentality and restore peace to our world, we must start where the separation began. We must regain our union with God through the pathway He has ordained—the atoning work of Christ.

"Having predestinated us unto the adoption of children by Jesus Christ to himself, according to the good pleasure of his will, to the praise of the glory of his grace, wherein he hath made us accepted in the beloved. In whom we have redemption through his blood, the forgiveness of sins, according to the riches of his grace" (Eph 1:5-7).

When we realize that God has "made us accepted in the beloved" with the subsequent benefits of redemption and forgiveness, we are encouraged to "come boldly into His presence and find mercy and Grace to help in time of need" (Heb 4:16). That atonement is not only to escape hell but more so to reestablish our Holy relationship with God which then establishes our peace with God.

Once we enter a holy relationship with God, we are ready to deal with the second area of division—the division within ourselves. When we sin, we violate our moral conscience and fall into self-condemnation. Since we cannot rid ourselves of our moral conscience and all its negative consequences, the only alternative is to stop sinning. How daunting is that? The average Christian would love to stop sinning but finds it impossible through self-effort. Even Paul tried to stop but ended up saying, "O wretched man that I am! Who shall deliver me from this body of death?" (Rom 7:24) He answers that question in the next verse by saying, "I thank God through Jesus Christ, our Lord." God has never asked us to cleanse ourselves of our sins through self-effort. He said He would do it. All He requires of us is to confess (own) our sins when we are made aware of them. He has promised to forgive us and *cleanse* that sin out of our lives (I Jn 1:9).

I remember back in my early days of pastoring, I struggled with my relationships with women. I could not look at a woman without impure thoughts filling my mind. It was a horrifying experience. How could a man of God pastor women with such thoughts flooding his mind? I hated myself. Finally, I got to the point where I cried out to God, saying, "God, if you don't change me, I'm out of here; I can't go on this way!"

Miraculously, God answered that cry and began a healing work in my life. His first step was to tell me to go to the back door of the sanctuary and greet people as they were leaving. I felt very uncomfortable shaking people's hands and responding to their kind words. It took me months to finally feel comfortable exchanging those simple acts of gratitude and affection. The second step in God's correction program occurred when a disabled young lady, who had adopted me as her big brother, preferred to give me a hug instead of a handshake. Very quickly, other women followed suit, and I found myself being hugged to death. Now, what do I do?

My best guess was to return the hug clumsily and hope I didn't offend them. It worked because the hugging continued and became the accepted form of affection at the door. I even hugged a few men, which met with varied levels of discomfort on their part. Some of them just froze up. It was almost hilarious, except for the fact that I knew what they were feeling. The ultimate result of all this hugging occurred when a woman came out of the service and informed me that she hadn't come to church that day for the sermon but for the hug.

The whole process of God's repair of my emotional and relational life took approximately one year. During that process, God showed me that because I had grown up in a family that expressed little or no affection, I grew up confusing affection with sexual activity. I didn't know that there was more than one way to interact with women personally. Since that experience, I have realized that many people suffer in their personal relationships due to being raised in a vacuum of positive affection. Happily, I can say that having learned this lesson, I now have great peace in expressing my love for both women and men through affection. I learned the importance of what Paul meant when he stated in Romans 12:10 that one of the marks of a transformed life is that we are "kindly affectioned one to another with brotherly love; in honor preferring one another." I can promise you that if you do not allow God to edit you of sin, you will end up like Paul and me and develop an extreme hatred—consciously or unconsciously--toward yourself, resulting in spiritual, mental, and physical damage. God made us, and only He knows how to fix us. Only through *His* cleansing of sin can we have a clear conscience and feel at peace with ourselves.

The final area of division, that division between people, is predicated upon the first two divisions. If we cannot find peace with God and ourselves, we will find it difficult, if not impossible, to have true peace with others. Jesus, however, gives us a solution to this dilemma. It is called love.

> "... thou shalt love the Lord thy God with all thy heart, and with all thy soul, and with all thy mind. This is the first and greatest commandment. And the second *is* like unto it; Thou shalt love thy neighbor as thyself." (Mat 22:37-39)

So, how do we find peace between ourselves and others? It starts with loving God, loving ourselves, and then loving others as ourselves. Without love, there is no peace. Loving God and ourselves is an absolute prerequisite to properly loving others. Paul explains how this works in Ephesians, chapter five.

> Eph 5:2 And walk in love, as Christ also hath loved us, and hath given himself for us an offering and a sacrifice to God for a sweet smelling savour.

> Eph 5:25 Husbands, love your wives, even as Christ also loved the church, and gave himself for it;

There is a right and a wrong way to love people. The right way is not to give ourselves to people for God but to give ourselves to God *for* people. If we give ourselves *to* people, we are giving them control of our lives, and that will produce co-dependent relationships that are not healthy. You cannot give yourself to others and depend on them to make you happy and fulfilled. True happiness comes only from the Lord. Giving ourselves to God for others is the only way to hope to have healthy relationships and find peace with others.

Most people see peace in the world as impossible. However, peace on earth is God's great Christmas promise: "Peace on earth, goodwill toward men." But can we trust the promises of God? Can we have faith that His prophecies are accurate predictions of the future? In the book of Isaiah, God states to the people of Israel that prophecy sets Him apart as God.

> "Remember the former things of old: for I *am* God, and *there is* none else; *I am* God, and *there is* none like me, declaring the end from the beginning, and from ancient times *the things* that are not *yet* done, saying, My counsel shall stand, and I will do all my pleasure:" (Isa 46:9,10)

In this scripture, God asks the Israelites to remember His promises to their ancestor, Abraham, which prove He is God. In Genesis fifteen, he promised Abraham that his descendants would be like the sands on the seashore and the stars of the sky but that they would first spend four hundred years as strangers in a land, not their own (Egypt). He is saying only God can forecast the future and make it happen. The idols that they worshipped could not do that.

Throughout history, God has made many prophetic statements concerning His plan for humanity. Many of those are Old Testament prophecies about Christ's first advent to the earth. They are exact in their content even though they were stated hundreds of years before their fulfillment. Here are a few of them.

> **Prophecy**: Isa 7:14 Therefore the Lord himself shall give you a sign; Behold, a virgin shall conceive, and bear a son, and shall call his name Immanuel.

> **Fulfillment:** Luk 1:35 And the angel answered and said unto her, The Holy Ghost shall come upon thee, and the power of the Highest shall overshadow thee: therefore, also that holy thing which shall be born of thee shall be called the Son of God.

Prophecy: Mic 5:2 But thou, Bethlehem Ephratah, *though* thou be little among the thousands of Judah, *yet* out of thee shall he come forth unto me *that is* to be ruler in Israel; whose goings forth *have been* from of old, from everlasting.

Fulfillment: Mat 2:4 And when he (Herod) had gathered all the chief priests and scribes of the people together, he demanded of them where Christ should be born.

Mat 2:5 And they said unto him, In Bethlehem of Judaea: for thus it is written by the prophet,

Mat 2:6 And thou Bethlehem, *in* the land of Juda, art not the least among the princes of Juda: for out of thee shall come a Governor, that shall rule my people, Israel.

Prophecy Psa 22:16 For dogs have compassed me: the assembly of the wicked have enclosed me: they pierced my hands and my feet.:

Fulfillment: Joh 19:37 And again another scripture saith, they shall look on him whom they pierced.

Prophecy: Psa 69:21 They gave me also gall for my meat; and in my thirst they gave me vinegar to drink.

Fulfillment: Mat 27:34 They gave him vinegar to drink mingled with gall: and when he had tasted *thereof,* he would not drink.

The apostle Peter writes in his last letter to the church that prophecy is like the headlights on a car or a strong flashlight that pierces the darkness ahead of us so that we can see what is coming. We will need that light's assistance until the rising sun shows us the reality of the coming day.

"We have also a more sure word of prophecy; whereunto ye do well that ye take heed, as unto a light that shineth in a dark place, until the day dawn, and the day star arise in your hearts:" (2Pe 1:19)

No, we do not have peace on earth today, but we have the beautiful light of that Christmas promise of peace that gives us hope. If God said it, it will happen. Holiness will someday blossom into peace on earth.

"Blessed and *holy is* he that hath part in the first resurrection: on such the second death hath no power, but they shall be priests of God and of Christ and shall reign with him a thousand years." (Rev 20:6 emphasis mine)

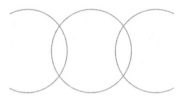

CHAPTER 15

OUR OBSESSION WITH RIGHTEOUSNESS

The Bible states that "there is none righteous, no not one" (Rom 3:10). Consciously or unconsciously, we know that we come short of God's standard, and because of that, there is in all of us a sense of guilt and fear of God plaguing us twenty-four-seven. Failure to fulfill God's standard and the resulting guilt has resulted in dangerous consequences in our lives and the Church. In our lives, this guilt is exceptionally destructive to the health of our minds and bodies, causing us to find ways to quiet its effects on us. Our obsession with righteousness in the Church always leads to a "works" theology based on rules that few can keep and many doctrines that do nothing but divide the Church. It also causes people and churches to compare themselves with others, which is nothing more than pride.

Before I go on, I need to state that it was never God's intent that we even be aware of righteousness. God's only prohibition to Adam and Eve was that they not eat of the tree of the knowledge of good and evil. Incredible as it may seem, He was saying He did not want them to guide their lives by a moral conscience but rather by a holy relationship with Him in which they acted according to His will and out of obedience to His commands. He said that eating the fruit of that tree, or appropriating a moral conscience, would result in death–and it has. Psychologists tell us that all sickness, disease, and premature death are brought about many times by faulty belief systems like "it runs in our family" or "everybody is getting it," empowered by conscious or unconscious guilt. Disease and death are fail-proof ways to punish and destroy ourselves for our "sins." Yet, it does not free us of sin. Punishment has a minimal effect on changing behavior, but it is still the favorite remedy for all evils. "He who sins must be punished" is the mantra of human nature. However, as Christ showed us in the parable of the prodigal son, it is not the mind of God.

Our attempts to mitigate the pain of guilt can also cause inappropriate behavior on our part. One of the most used actions to soothe the pain of guilt is to blame someone else for our behavior, thereby justifying ourselves. Adam's cry after eating the fruit was, "That woman you gave me made me do it." If we can transfer a share of our guilt to someone else, we can feel some sense of relief. However, we must continue to blame others if we want continued comfort. Blaming allows us to vent our anger on someone else rather than ourselves. Blaming and the resulting conflicts are the major causes of marital discord. In their attempt to punish each other, spouses will have affairs, overspend, gamble, withhold sex, stop talking, flirt, gossip, get into screaming matches, abuse one another, get divorced, or sometimes even resort to murder. On a social and political level, politicians always find someone to blame for the disorders we are experiencing, which is never themselves. Democrats blame the Republicans, and Republicans blame the Democrats. Hitler found it very convenient to blame the Jews for Germany's dire economic conditions after World War I. Likewise, we in the United States have found it very convenient to blame people with darker skin for destroying our moral and economic values in America. In 2020, hate crimes against Latino, African, and Asian Americans skyrocketed. Blaming people of a different heritage causes us to stop looking for the real reasons for our malaise and proper solutions to the problem.

A closely related technique is to project our guilt onto others and judge them. To understand projection, we can look at a movie projector. Any image in the projector, whether on film or digital, is projected onto a blank screen, giving the illusion that the image on the screen is real. The image has nothing to do with the screen but exposes the image in the projector. In the same way, we can project feelings and thoughts of guilt onto other people and be under the illusion that they have our problems. Now, we can judge them and not ourselves. The angry person tends to see people around him as angry and threatening. A fearful person sees a terrifying world. A proud person sees a competitive and critical world. An apathetic person sees a hopeless world. An unforgiving person sees both unforgiving people and an unforgiving God. Christ summarized these phenomena quite well in the following verses.

> "And why do you look on the splinter that is in your brother's eye, but do not consider the beam that is in your own eye? Or how will you say to your brother, Let me pull the splinter out of your eye, and, behold, a beam *is* in your own eye? Hypocrite! First, cast the beam out of your own eye, and then you shall see clearly to cast the splinter out of your brother's eye" (Mat 7:3-5).

> "Judge not, and you shall not be judged. Condemn not, and you shall not be condemned. Forgive, and you shall be forgiven" (Luk 6:37).

Paul adds, "To the pure, all things are pure, but to those who are defiled and unbelieving, nothing is pure, but even their mind and conscience are defiled" (Tit 1:15). Dr. David Hawkins, MD, Ph.D. clinically verified this phenomenon through consciousness research. In his Map of Consciousness, He shows how our level of consciousness, such as peace, joy, anger, fear, grief, etc, affects how we view our world and God.[18]

Another way many people mitigate guilt is to overindulge in activities that produce sensual pleasure. They overeat, overdrink, overwork,

---

[18] David R Hawkins, Apendix A,"Lettin go, The Path to Surrender", Hay House Inc.

overplay, overspend, oversleep, smoke, and get involved in drugs or anything else that allows them to escape the pain and deny reality. Unfortunately, these behaviors do not absolve guilt but add to it. Though conditioned by social norms, our minds and bodies cannot escape the ruthless condemnation imposed by a guilty conscience.

Suppression and repression are other popular ways of dealing with guilt. We push guilt into our subconscious so we won't have to think about it. In doing so, we may absolve the mind of some guilt, but it still impacts the body. Suppressed guilt may be the most dangerous form of guilt. When guilt is suppressed, its destructive force has free reign to wreak havoc on our health.

It is essential to recognize that mitigating guilt in these ways is more destructive than helpful. The critical issue in dealing with guilt is to *own it*. However, I realize that acknowledging our guilt is easier said than done. As I have said, many people feel that punishment is the only remedy for our guilt. Therefore, we must find people who do *not* share that belief before we morally expose ourselves. Within the Church, James says we should confess our faults to each other so that we may pray for each other (James 5:16). John adds that we can confess our sins to God, who assures us that He will always forgive and cleanse us from our sins (I John 1:9). These men are saying that, in the Church, God has provided a way that we can positively deal with sin. It's called Holiness.

I believe the purpose of the atonement is more about abolishing our sense of guilt than appeasing the wrath of a righteous God. Because of guilt, we think God *must* punish us. We should remind ourselves that the prodigal's father did not punish him by putting him in the pig pen. He put himself there. It is our fear and shame that separates us from God. Christ died to remove the veil of guilt between God and us so that we would feel free to seek a holy relationship with God. In securing a holy relationship with God and the body of Christ, we can feel safe to expose our sins. The good news is that God has done everything He can to make that relationship possible for us through the atoning work of Christ. There is nothing more He can do. We must believe and receive God's remedy. Many believers assume that the only reason for Christ's death on the cross was to appease a righteous God. If He was only a righteous God, that might be true. However, He is also a holy God. Isaiah described Him as the "Holy One of Israel," seeking harmonious relationships with His children at all costs. The angels circle the throne, crying, "Holy, Holy." God is righteous, but I believe His most outstanding virtue is Holiness. He is unified within the trinity and desires to be one with us as well. Only in the security of that holy relationship can we successfully deal with the destructive results of guilt.

> "Let us draw near with a true heart in full assurance of faith, having our hearts sprinkled from an evil conscience (guilt), and our bodies washed with pure water" (Heb 10:22, emphasis mine). (Heb_10:22).

Because of Christ's atoning act, we can come boldly before His throne of grace and find help in times of need. (Heb 4:16) The writer of Hebrews goes on to say:

> "By a new and living way, which he hath consecrated for us, through the veil, that is to say, his flesh" (Heb 10:12)

If you doubt the sentiments I've expressed in the above paragraph, you must read and study the seventeenth chapter of the gospel of John. In this chapter, John is writing about the last intercessory prayer of Christ before He was crucified. I think that prayer expresses the most profound thoughts and desires of Jesus' Heart concerning His crucifixion and what it would achieve. However, suppose chapter seventeen was not in the Bible, and we were left to guess the sentiments of that prayer. In that case, I think the average Christian, because of guilt, would conclude that Jesus was asking that His death would be adequate to appease God's wrath against sinners and keep us out of hell. Jesus did not die to free us from the consequences of sin so that we could go merrily on sinning with no consequences. That's called "antinomianism," or cheap grace. He died to free us from sin *itself* through a holy relationship with God.

> "But now being made free from sin and become servants
> to God, ye have your fruit unto Holiness, and the end
> everlasting life." (Rom 6:22)

There is nothing said there about righteousness or hell. It's all about
being one with God and each other. That's Holiness.

> "Neither pray I for these alone, but for them also which
> shall believe on me through their word; That they all
> may be one; as thou, Father, *art* in me, and I in thee,
> that they also may be one in us: that the world may be-
> lieve that thou hast sent me. And the glory which thou
> gavest me I have given them; that they may be one, even
> as we are one: I in them, and thou in me, that they may
> be made perfect in one; and that the world may know
> that thou hast sent me, and hast loved them, as thou
> hast loved me." (Joh 17:20-23)

In our obsession with righteousness, evangelism has become a practice of using our fear and guilt to motivate salvation. One lady com-
mented to my wife that she doesn't feel like she has been to Church unless she walks out feeling guilty. But I don't think the Church's purpose
is to make us feel guilty. We already have enough guilt. Shouldn't the
gospel introduce us to a way of life where we can live free of sin and guilt?
I'm not saying that hell is not real and scary, but living a life in Holiness
with the Creator of the universe is a much more positive reason to receive
Christ as your savior. The gospel, or good news, is about so much more
than going to Heaven rather than hell when we die. It is about experiencing Kingdom realities now, though not to the same degree we will
experience them later. One of my favorite sayings is, "You don't have to
wait for Heaven to have a heavenly life."

I once asked a young lady if she had ever accepted Christ. Her
answer didn't surprise me, but it did disappoint me. She said, "Sure, I
don't want to go to hell." As I watch her and many other Christians, I
don't see the mitigation of their guilt; worse yet, I don't observe the joy

of their salvation. I see these people continuing their lives after accepting Christ with little change in their daily walk, except that they may be more religious. Religion can often give the illusion of Holiness but also hide one's lack of living in the reality of Holiness. They never seem to experience the joy, peace, and power of being a child of God. Their guilt will not allow them to get too close to God. Except for times of crisis, it is more comfortable to keep God at a distance from our daily lives. He is still scary to them, not their "Abba" father. They can never come boldly before the throne of grace, and they will struggle significantly to experience Holiness.

As a pastor, I have officiated at more funerals than I can remember. Families always hope their loved ones are in Heaven. It's tough, if not impossible, to tell a family at a funeral that their loved one could be in hell. The closest I've gotten to that statement was when I said, "If you don't enjoy God here on earth, you are not going enjoy heaven because that's God's home." Speaking the truth in love on such an occasion is extremely hard. If people only want to go to Heaven because they don't want to go to hell, they could experience shell shock upon entering Heaven. Heaven will seem like a really long church service–especially with all those angels flying around singing "Holy, Holy, Holy." Holiness is the hallmark of Heaven. It is a place of complete unity with God and His children. Maybe if I wish to prepare people for Heaven, I should preach more about Holiness here on earth and less on condemnation. Perhaps I should talk more about walking in the spirit (Holiness) rather than just living in the Spirit (Gal 5:25). Maybe we should find ways to walk in unity with the rest of the body of Christ and not nit-pick over every little wind of doctrine (Eph 4:13, 14). Maybe we should reach out in love to other churches in the community rather than try to compete with them. Christ said that unity in the Church is the best evidence that His Father sent Him to this earth and that God loves the world (Joh 17:23). Holiness, not legalistic condemnation, provides an alternative lifestyle to a divided world.

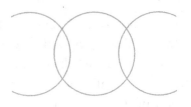

CHAPTER 16

TREATING SYMPTOMS

Every malady in life has two aspects: a cause and an effect manifesting in symptoms. Symptoms are the first indication that something has occurred but can't easily be traced back to a cause.

The medical and mental health professions concentrate most of their practice on managing the symptoms of a disease rather than eliminating their causes. There are two reasons for this. First, the symptoms often kill rather than the disease itself. Secondly, determining and eliminating causes is more challenging than dealing with symptoms. For example, bacteria and viruses are the cause of many diseases. They can cause fevers, infection, inflammation, and respiratory problems, which can, in. turn, destroy the body if not mitigated. Medical science has successfully treated the symptoms of bacteria and viruses, saving many lives. However, science has had a more challenging time finding ways of destroying certain bacteria and viruses once they have entered the body. It has developed antibiotics that have proven successful in eliminating a wide variety of bacteria in the body; however, it has had less success in producing antibodies to kill viruses. Therefore, the common cold is still very common. Ultimately, the body's immune system must destroy the bacteria or viruses once they enter the body. Thus, science must find ways to strengthen or supplement that system.

In 2021, thousands were fighting for their lives due to the Covid 19 virus. However, they were treated primarily for respiratory and other symptoms, not the virus. Later, doctors cloned an antibody (monoclonal) that proved helpful in fighting the virus if introduced into the body soon after infection. But until the virus could be eliminated, they treated the patients with drugs to curb their reactions, sometimes having to put them on a ventilator to help them survive until the battle was over. If the antibodies destroyed the virus, the patient lived. If the virus won, they would die.

In the mental health field, the healing of mental illness is more elusive than the healing of physical ailments because the causes are more likely to be rooted in our past experiences, values, and belief systems than in physical reasons. Past abuse and trauma can affect our minds in ways that elude easy cures. If the symptoms of mental illness are severe, drugs are needed to protect the patient from self-inflicted harm. Actual cures may never be found.

The criminal justice system also deals almost exclusively with the symptoms or the expressions of crime rather than the causes of the crime. Many crimes result from mental illness; however, other roots of crime lie more deeply embedded within human nature and in systems that humans have promulgated, such as prejudice and indifference to human rights. Because human nature has separated itself from God, it has lost its ability to guide itself in a morally acceptable manner. The prophet Jeremiah expressed the results of this separation quite clearly when he stated, "O LORD, I know that the way of man *is* not in himself: *it is* not in man that walketh to direct his steps" (Jer 10:23). The Bible states that we are all sinners. "We have all sinned and come short of the glory of God" (Rom 3:23). This fallen nature, or separation from God, is the ultimate cause of all sin, Whether it be a crime or a dysfunctional relationship. Another way of saying this is that sins are symptoms of a lack of holiness or intimate connection with God. I want to re-emphasize that holiness is not just a matter of avoiding sin but cultivating a relationship in which sin will have less opportunity to manifest and cause harm.

When God created humans, He created them in His image, or like Himself, with the intention that His desire to be in a relationship with us would be reciprocated (or mirrored) by our desire to be in a relationship with Him. Jesus described the nature of this relationship with God in the following statements;

> "Verily, verily, I say unto you, The Son can do nothing of himself, but what he seeth the Father do: for what things soever he doeth, these also doeth the Son likewise." (Joh 5:19)

> "I can of mine own self do nothing: as I hear, I judge: and my judgment is just; because I seek not mine own will, but the will of the Father which hath sent me." (Joh 5:30)

> "I do nothing of myself; but as my Father hath taught me, I speak these things." (Joh 8:28)

> "As the Father knoweth me, even so, know I the Father:" (Joh_10:15)

> "And I know that his commandment is life everlasting: whatsoever I speak therefore, even as the Father said unto me, so I speak." (Joh_12:50)

> "But that the world may know that I love the Father; and as the Father gave me commandment, even so I do." (Joh_14:31)

As we look at the world's condition today, we should not give up trying to mitigate the symptoms of our broken relationship with God. If we did give up, I fear our planet could self-destruct relatively quickly. We may have to seek medical help and rely on the appropriate use of drugs to cope with disease symptoms. We must also continue incarcerating criminals when it is necessary to stop evil forces from destroying humanity. These measures are helpful and indeed not sinful, but they do not address the ultimate cause of our human pain and dysfunction– *our separation from God*. Suppose we accept that our separation from God or lack of holiness is the root cause of our earthly disorders. In that case, it should be clear that people cannot satisfactorily address peace and unity in the world independent from God. Without God, we can only address the symptoms, not the cause.

The good news is that God does have a solution to our dilemma. We don't have to struggle with managing symptoms by ourselves. He desires a holy relationship with us and has provided a way through His Son to recover that sacred relationship. We don't have to solve the earth's problems alone. He gives us a great promise in Rev 21:5: *"Behold, I make all things new. And he said unto me, Write: for these words are true and faithful."* Only God can eliminate the cause of sin and all of its symptoms. Therefore, it behooves us to seek that holy relationship with God if we genuinely want to find solutions to our lack of physical, mental, and social health.

Simply being religious does not satisfy the criteria of being holy. God states through Isaiah that holiness comes from spending time with God in intimate fellowship. He called that time "Sabbath." Religion has, in most cases, lost the significance of the Sabbath and turned it into a day of religious activity characterized by attending church. If we sincerely seek, value, and practice holiness as Isaiah portrays, He will put us on a high road. Isaiah describes it this way.

> "If thou turn away thy foot from (because of) the sabbath, *from* doing thy pleasure on my holy day; and call the sabbath a delight, the holy of the LORD, honorable; and shalt honor him, not doing thine own ways, nor finding thine own pleasure, nor speaking *thine own* words: Then shalt thou delight thyself in the LORD, and I will cause thee to ride upon the high places of the earth, and feed thee with the heritage of Jacob, thy father: for the mouth of the LORD hath spoken *it.* " (Is 58:13,14)

God gave the Sabbath to Israel as a time to converse with God on an intimate, holy level in which God could point out their errors and guide them toward a good life. If we are open to Him, God will reveal the spiritual roots or causes of our problems and help us eliminate those causes, not just manage their symptoms.

> "If we confess our sins, he is faithful and just to forgive us *our* sins, and to *cleanse us* from all unrighteousness." (1Jn 1:9, emphasis mine)

To help validate some of the statements I've made concerning spiritual causes of physical and mental symptoms, I would like to draw from the writings of two men who have studied the spirit-medical-physical relationship in detail. The first is Dr. Henry Wright of the "Be in Health" organization, a pastor who approaches the relationship from both Biblical and medical research. The second is the late Dr. David R. Hawkins, a noted psychiatrist who explored this relationship from a clinical perspective.

Dr. Wright states: "It has been my experience that about 80 percent of all incurable diseases have spiritual root issues with corresponding psychological and biological manifestations."[19] He goes on to say:

> "Disease follows relationship breakdown. Relationship breakdown involves separation on three levels. 1) Separation from the Godhead. Many of you don't have your peace with God the Father. 2) Separation from yourself. Many people don't like themselves. .... 3) Separation from others. This could be due to bitterness, envy, and jealousy, or it could be anger or fear of another."[20]

This breakdown of relationships constitutes a degeneration of holiness with God and other humans. The Bible declares a very close correlation between our relationship with God and with people.

When discussing the spiritual causes of the physical and mental

---

[19] Wright, Henry W. "A More Excellent Way". Whitaker House. Kindle Edition.
[20] Ibid.

diseases we may experience, I want to be very careful. Many Christians either have never explored that relationship or don't believe such a relationship exists. In failing to look for spiritual causes of sickness within, we conclude that illness and disease are inflicted on us from the outside. Under this mentality, we tend to see ourselves as victims of the world around us. The fact that Jesus claims he has overcome the world should give us hope that our environment does not have the power to afflict sickness and disease on people; however, few people share that hope. Both Wright and Hawkins agree that we do leave the door open to illness when we have unresolved spiritual issues and broken relationships in our lives. Wright calls these issues "sin," while Hawkins calls them "faulty belief systems." The Apostle Paul connects these terms–sin and faulty belief systems– when he says, "whatsoever is not of faith is sin." (Rom 12:23)

In addition to sins and faulty belief systems, all illnesses have an underlying element of unconscious guilt. Hawkins states:

"All these illnesses (which he examined clinically) came about as the result of belief systems and were also accompanied to some degree by unconscious guilt. ….. If we have a physical illness, we can just presume correctly that there is unconscious guilt."[21](emphasis mine)

Guilt unconsciously causes us to accept illness as punishment for our sins. All humanity believes that evil must be punished. So, what better way is there to punish ourselves for our sense of guilt than by suffering physically? The Bible also says that guilt inhibits our faith.

"Holding faith, and a good conscience; which some having put away concerning faith have made shipwreck:" (1Ti 1:19)

---

[21] Hawkins, David R.. Healing and Recovery (pp. 418-419). Veritas Publishing. Kindle Edition.

"Holding the mystery of the faith in a pure conscience."
(1Ti 3:9)

Through Christ, we have the tools to ward off many, if not all, diseases with something other than drugs and doctors. However, most Christians are either unaware of those tools, do not believe in them, or do not know how to utilize them. Hosea stated that God's children are destroyed because of the lack of knowledge (Hos 4:6). Therefore, growing in the knowledge of God and all that we may claim in Christ should be the lifelong pursuit of all Christians. Paul declares in Philippians chapter three that he was still on that journey of apprehending truth and had not yet arrived. That is also true of me. However, the good news is that God has given us the Holy Spirit to guide us in this journey.

"Howbeit when he, the Spirit of truth, is come, he will (1) guide you into all truth: for he shall not speak of himself; but whatsoever he shall hear, *that* shall he speak: and (2) he will show you things to come. He shall glorify me: (3) *for he shall receive of mine, and shall show it unto you.* All things that the Father hath are mine: therefore said I, that *he shall take of mine, and shall show it unto you*". (Joh 16:13-15) (emphasis mine)

So, could most illnesses be traced to spiritual causes? A rather large and growing amount of medical evidence seems to confirm this idea. Dr. Hawkins, based on his clinical work, makes the incredible statement:

"In reality, we are not the victims of viruses, accidents, cholesterol, or imbalanced uric acid levels. When we re-own our own power, we say, "It's my mind that has been creating that."[22]

---

[22] Hawkins, David R.. Healing and Recovery (p. 105). Veritas Publishing. Kindle Edition.

However, blaming our environment for our sickness is much more acceptable to most folks than accepting responsibility for our ill health. The Bible says we must confess or own up to our faults before God can help us. (I John 1:9) It is hard to admit that we may have faulty belief systems (or sin). However, such an admission can free us to change the situation by changing our minds rather than our environment. We don't have to be limited to dealing with symptoms. Paul states that we empower ourselves to transform our lives by changing our minds. (Rom 12:2) But how does that happen? How do we change our minds to find a better life? It can only happen as we submit ourselves to holiness with God. In that intimate interaction with God, He will "renew our minds" and set us on that "high road." This is the only way to deal with the causes of our disorders rather than merely mitigate the symptoms. To me, that sounds like a worthy goal in life.

EPILOGUE

Today, while shopping at a large chain department store, I noticed the employees wore tee shirts with the slogan: "We are stronger together." This slogan resonates with many people because it is a truism. Unfortunately, it is dismissed by many as being merely a cliché, something one doesn't have to take seriously or put into action. Therefore, few people seek to build the kind of relationships the slogan expresses. I believe that somewhere in the human psyche, people know that working together can lead to a more prosperous life and that the whole is greater than the sum of its parts. Then why, I must ask, do so *few* people base their life actions on the practice of this truth? Paul sheds some light on the subject.

> "If then I do that which I would not, I consent unto the law that *it is* good. Now then, it is no more I that do it, but sin that dwelleth in me." (Rom 7:16,17)

Paul says something within us keeps us from doing what we know is right. He calls it sin. Now, sin means different things to different people, but to Paul, it meant anything that is not of faith (for whatsoever *is* not of faith is sin, Rom 14:23). Sin keeps us from trusting God, other people, and even our minds. Therefore, our fleshly self, or ego, operates only out of self–interest and usually produces very irrational behavior. Is it not irrational that humans who know that unity and working together is ultimately better choose to fight and oppose actions that favor corporate well-being over our individual preferences?

My first objective in writing this book was to show that holiness is not just an ethereal religious term but is God's overriding concept of how He has designed the universe. He designed all creation to reflect His nature as a triune God by creating it to work together in a proper working relationship, producing the best possible results for the whole. We see this in the natural world, where we observe how plant and animal life complement each other. We also see holiness in the human body, where some 50 trillion cells all relate to each other, under the direction of the head, to maintain and enhance the body as a whole. The apostle Paul may have been considering the concept of holiness in nature when stating that what we observe in nature should lead us to God. (Rom 1:20)

Holiness worked in the garden, but the world has been separated from God since the fall. AW Tozer describes the result of that fall quite accurately.

> "It is a truism to say that order in nature depends upon right relationships; to achieve harmony, each thing must be in its proper position relative to each other thing. In human life, it is not otherwise. I (Tozer) have hinted that the cause of all our human miseries is a radical moral dislocation, an upset in our relation to God and to each other. For whatever else the Fall may have been, it was most certainly a sharp change in man's relation to his Creator. He adopted toward God an altered attitude, and by so doing destroyed the proper Creator-creature relation in which, unknown to him, his true happiness lay."[23] (emphasis mine)

After the fall, God selected people who would submit to Him to restore holiness to the earth, beginning with Abram. God directed Abram's children, the Jews, to be a Holy nation; however, they failed Him. So, He sent His son Jesus to establish His Kingdom on earth made up of those persons who *would* submit to Christ and live in holiness. In

---

[23] Tozer, A. W. (Aiden Wilson). The Pursuit of God (p. 46). Kindle Edition.

his first letter to the church, John summarized what that holy kingdom would look like.

> "For the life was manifested, and we have seen *it,* and bear witness, and shew unto you that eternal life, which was with the Father, and was manifested unto us; that which we have seen and heard declare we unto you, that ye also may have fellowship with us: and truly our fellowship *is* with the Father, and with his Son Jesus Christ. And these things write we unto you, that your joy may be full. This then is the message which we have heard of him, and declare unto you, that God is light, and in him is no darkness at all. If we say that we have fellowship with him, and walk in darkness, we lie, and do not the truth: but if we walk in the light, as he is in the light, we have fellowship one with another, and the blood of Jesus Christ his Son cleanseth us from all sin. (I John 1:2-7)

John is saying that living a holy life with each other begins with a holy relationship with Christ. If we truly have that relationship with Christ, His Holy Spirit will teach us how to live with one another. "Submitting yourselves one to another in the fear of God." (Eph 5:21)

Adam and Eve knew nothing about managing a garden. Instead, they relied on the guidance of God, who knew everything about gardens and life. Today, we have a similar problem. We know little about managing our lives and getting along with others. Jeremiah points out that "*it is* not in man that walketh to direct his steps" (Jer 10:30). Likewise, Paul points out in the above scripture (Rom 7) that humans cannot trust their knowledge of right and wrong to do the right thing because they have a sinful nature. But today's world still insists we can effectively manage our lives using only our moral conscience as a guide." God told Adam and Eve that using a moral conscience rather than holiness to guide their lives would result in death—which it has. Mental health professionals tell us that the guilt of violating our moral conscience is the empowering force behind all sickness and premature death. It is also a significant condition that separates people from themselves, others, and God.

My second objective in writing this book was to develop a working definition of holiness. I don't remember ever a sermon or series of sermons on holiness. When I researched the subject, I found no clear and definitive explanation of holiness. I did find terms in the Bible and other religious books such as "walking in the Spirit," "unity," "Kingdom theology," and "the indwelling Christ," which touch on holiness without calling it holiness. For example, Andrew Murrey, in his discussion of the Kingdom, describes the Kingdom within us as:

> "God's manifested presence with us without ceasing; God's blessed rule and dominion over us established, so that His heavenly will is done in us and by us; God's mighty power descending upon us, so that through us Christ can do His work of saving souls."[24]

That is the best working definition of holiness I have ever found; however, he never calls it holiness.

My third objective in writing this book was to clarify the relationship between holiness and righteousness. If we explain holiness as moral purity, it is beyond our reach since we are not morally pure. Moral purity is absolute righteousness, and the Bible declares none righteous. (Rom 3:10) However, if you define holiness instead as relational purity, it seems more possible for us to attain it. Relational purity is a commitment to unity and fidelity with God and others, such as spouses and followers of Christ. This kind of relationship can have a powerful cleansing and transforming effect on our lives. In short, holiness is not righteousness, yet it will produce righteousness.

If you explore the first four of the Ten Commandments, you will find that they have more to do with relational purity than righteousness

---

[24] Murray, Andrew. The Kingdom of God is Within You (p. 13). Ichthus Publications. Kindle Edition.

or moral purity. Briefly stated, they are as follows: Thou shall have no other gods before God.

1. Don't worship idols because He is a jealous God and doesn't want to compete with objects of His creation for your worship.
2. Do not belittle God but treat Him with respect.
3. Take time from your daily schedules to spend time with God. That is "Holy" time, or time set aside to build that holy relationship.

These are the same desires any married person would desire of their spouse, for they are the framework of a holy and fulfilling relationship. Sin can destroy a holy relationship if not addressed. However, if we acknowledge the presence of sin in our lives and let God deal with it in the context of that relationship, it need not destroy us. (I Jn 1:9) The only thing that can ruin holiness is willfully denying God entrance into our lives, leaving God no option but to deny us. "If we suffer, we shall also reign with *him:* if we deny *him,* he also will deny us: If we believe not, *yet* he abideth faithful: he cannot deny himself." (2 Tim 2:12,13)

> "They profess that they know God; but in works they deny *him,* being abominable, and disobedient, and unto every good work reprobate." (Tit 1:16)

Maybe a quick final story can summarize the point I'm trying to make concerning holiness and righteousness. Once, I invited a fishing buddy of mine to church. He responded, "Well, I've got a lot of problems, and when I deal with those, I will consider attending church." So, I asked him a simple question. "When do we clean our fish, before or after we catch them?" He responded, "After,"– to which I replied, "So does God."

Printed in the United States
by Baker & Taylor Publisher Services